"THEY PROBABLY LIED"

AN ANATOMY OF A REAL ESTATE FRAUD AND HOW TO AVOID BECOMING A VICTIM

Jack Rudolph and Michael Huntley

ISBN: 978-1-4834-9021-2 (sc)
ISBN: 978-1-4834-9022-9 (hc)
ISBN: 978-1-4834-9032-8 (e)

Library of Congress Control Number: 2018909975

Lulu Publishing Services rev. date: 12/04/2019

Although the accounts of this book took place in the state of Texas the laws are very similar from state to state with subtle exceptions. The "Tips" we've provided are however universal.

"Jack and Michael hit the nail on the head. Their book should be a must read for buyers, sellers, real estate agents and anyone looking to be armed with the necessary tools to make sound investment decisions, avoiding the pitfalls and ultimately be on their way to successful wealth building."

Jack Rockwell, P.A.
President of Investment Services
TRG Investment Real Estate, LLC

"They Probably Lied" has some valuable lessons, some of which I've experienced myself. I've recommended this book to the students in my Gold Club".

Ron LeGrand.

"The Probably Lied" is an excellent choice for any beginning multi-family investor. The Tips will save you time, money and heartache. Reading through these tips brought back some many memories from my early deals because I made many of the mistakes the Tips help you to avoid. Tip 48 is a tip that only an experienced investor would know. I use this Tip as a way to stop small problems become big problems.

David Lindahl
Author "Multi Family Millions"
Good luck with the book!

THE FORWARD

As a seasoned real estate investor and multifamily broker, I have read dozens of books on real estate investing. Every single one of them is nearly identical, "this is the story of how I became successful.""They Probably Lied," is the opposite; "this is how I lost everything and this is what I learned." It is the most eye opening book I have read to date on Real Estate Investing. Jack Rudolph and Michael Huntley tell their story of how their nest egg and life's savings vanished overnight after they purchased a seemingly too good to be true apartment complex.

Wether you're buying your first investment property or you're a seasoned pro, there are valuable lessons to be had from Jack and Michael's catastrophic loss.

Adam Smith
Broker
HFO Investment Real Estate LLC

Dedication

I am dedicating this book to my father who spent hundreds of hours going over the details of this case with me and even more helping me to write this book. He gave me two of the greatest gifts one could ever give his time and his love.

-Jack Rudolph

CONTENTS

FTBD

Definition of Fraud

"Chapter 27 of the Texas Business and Commerce Code provides an additional remedy to persons who are victims of fraud in connection with real estate and stock transactions. The elements of statutory fraud are essentially the same as common-law fraud, except to establish statutory fraud the plaintiff does not have to prove the defendant's knowledge or recklessness.

"To bring an action for statutory fraud, the plaintiff must establish that there was fraud in connection with a transaction involving real estate, stock in a corporation or stock in a joint-stock company. A transaction means that there is either a sale of real estate or a stock or there was a contract to sell real estate or stock entered into between the parties. Real estate includes land, the structures or improvements on the land and any assets of the real estate, such as minerals and water. A transaction involving the purchase of a stock option, however, is not considered a transaction involving stock in a corporation under Chapter 27."

"To prevail in an action for statutory fraud, the plaintiff must prove that the defendant:

1. Made a false representation of past or existing material fact,
2. Made a false promise to do an act, or
3. *Benefited by not disclosing that a third party's representation or promise was false.*

"The proof of the element of a false representation of past or existing material fact is the same for common-law and statutory fraud. A false promise must be material and made with the intent to not fulfill it. *A claim of nondisclosure may be established by showing the defendant had actual awareness that the third-party's representation was false, did not disclose this to the plaintiff and the defendant benefited from the non-disclosure. Actual awareness may be inferred when objective manifestations indicate that the defendant was actually aware that his actions were false, deceptive or unfair."*

"The plaintiff must also prove that the false promise was made prior to entering into a contract and for the purpose of inducing the plaintiff to enter into the contract. This element can be shown by establishing that the defendant either intended that the plaintiff enter into the contract or had reason to believe that the plaintiff would enter into the contract in reliance on the representation. The element of reliance is the same for both common-law and statutory fraud.

"The plaintiff must further prove that the false representation or promise caused injury or damages. In an action for statutory fraud, a plaintiff may recover both actual and exemplary damages. To recover exemplary damages from a defendant who made a false representation, the plaintiff must prove, by clear and convincing evidence, that the defendant had actual awareness of the falsity of the representation. When the action involves non-disclosure concerning third parties, the plaintiff must prove, by clear and convincing evidence, that the defendant had actual awareness of the falsity of the third party's promise or representation in order to recover exemplary damages."

It is our intent through this book to prove that the strong circumstantial evidence presented to the reader shows the agents involved should have known the financial information we had been provided in this transaction was false and may have even had a hand in preparing it. Not only did the circumstances behind this sale meet the aforementioned definition of fraud, but it was so egregious that it warranted exemplary damages. Yet we lost the case and were unable to prevail in the forthcoming litigation. It is our goal to use the turmoil from this transaction to encourage future real estate buyers to do as much due diligence as possible before proceeding into any transaction. It is a lot easier to not close on a purchase than it is to leave your fate in the hands of a jury. All of the names of people and places have been changed to protect identities.

CHARACTER

Character cannot be developed in ease and quiet. Only through experience of trial and suffering can the soul be strengthened, ambition inspired, and success achieved.
—Helen Keller

Michael and I considered ourselves to be men of character and integrity, but we were naïve in believing that all men and women operated under the same set of standards.

THE START OF IT ALL

It was the late 2000s. People had been making money buying and selling properties hand over fist for the five years of the new millennium, Michael and I included, but little did we know our bubble was about to burst.

"They probably lied?" I kept saying to myself repeatedly as Garrett's words resonated in my head.

"Was he kidding?"

How could Garrett have said so flippantly, without hesitation that his clients had, probably lied to us?

Garrett Brewer and Isaac Davis were agents for Daniel and June Feng who sold us the Crestview apartments, a sixty-six unit apartment complex in Corpus Christi, Texas.

What did he mean by that? I had just finished telling him that Michael and I had lost nearly a quarter of a million dollars in less than one year of ownership of this apartment complex. I told him that we could not even collect enough to cover the utility bills as he had told me his clients were doing while we were in escrow with them. We had lost two hundred and fifty thousand dollars and were on the verge of bankruptcy and all they could say was "Eh, they (the Feng's) probably lied"?

If they did feel their clients were not telling the truth why had they not been more cautious when disseminating their financial statements to the public? Now mind you, this was not a little white lie, like fudging a name or two on the rent roll, but one so horrific that it put two unsuspecting buyers on the verge of financial ruin.

We just kept thinking to ourselves "How could they have lied to us"? We counted on the income they had reported to us during the due diligence period as part of our decision to purchase the Crestview. We relied on this income to cover the payment on the $1.5 million in financing we took out to purchase this property. This was a loan that was backed by the performance of the property and it was based on this performance we signed a personal guarantee. A guarantee which was backed by our personal assets and the homes in which our families lived.

It was this one conversation that was the basis of what turned out to be a major fraud case and a two-year forensic analysis of everything we'd been told about or given on the Crestview Apartments. Michael and I figured that after all, if the Fengs lied about collecting the money from their tenants for their utility bills, what else could they have lied about?

However, I digress. Let me tell you a little bit about me and my business partner and best friend, with whom I made this investment. My name is Jack Rudolph, and my business partner is Michael Huntley. I am a sales representative in the high-tech industry in Orange County, and Michael works for the Planning Department in Los Angeles County. We are not a corporation, we are not wealthy, and we are not real estate moguls. Labels we would use to describe ourselves would be dad, husband, coach, scout leader, church volunteer.

We were just two people who were seeking the American dream for our families, a way to put our kids through school, a way to have a comfortable retirement and perhaps a path to self-realization. We are writing this story not in an effort to win sympathy for our cause but in order to help other investors avoid the pitfalls of real estate fraud. Real estate is, in most cases, a great investment, and we have done very well in real estate both together and individually.

However, in this particular case we did not.

TIP 1

If it sounds too good to be true, it probably is.

The story of the nightmare known as the Crestview Apartments began in the fall of 2006. Michael and I had just sold a small apartment building we owned in downtown Reno and needed to roll over the proceeds of our investment into another property; otherwise, we'd be liable for the capital gain taxes associated with it. Through an Internet solicitation we received from Colonial Properties, which touted itself as the largest seller of apartment complexes in the United States, I was sent a listing for a sixty-six-unit complex in Corpus Christi, Texas. It was known as the Crestview Apartments. The property was listed at $1.73 million and boasted not only 95 percent occupancy but 95 percent *paid* occupancy. This is typically unheard of, particularly since it was in a C- or D-type neighborhood of blue-collar, lower-income clientele. This should have been our first sign that something was wrong. A scenario such as this is typically unheard of in larger C-class properties. Ordinarily with these types of apartments, you have some people who are down on their luck, lose a job, and are unable to pay rent.

Beware of sellers reporting financials that are too good to be true, especially if the property has been on the market for more than a week and no one has it under contract!

TIP 2

Always insist on more than one piece of verifiable income.

The Crestview was comprised of one-, two-, and three-bedroom units near a major shipping port in the Gulf of Mexico and close to the Texas Walmart distribution center. The rents were listed as below market, which Michael researched and verified. This sounded like the perfect property for us. It was a chance to move up to a larger property than the twenty-unit complex we had just sold in Reno. The Crestview Apartments was owned by Daniel and June Feng, two Chinese immigrants who held the property in the name of their LLC, Shanghai Investments. The principal agents for Colonial Properties were Isaac Davis and Garrett Brewer. During the due diligence period, Michael and I were sent some very impressive financial statements by Isaac Davis.

As part of our due diligence, we asked for the Fengs' bank statements and tax returns. Garrett Brewer, who was now our main contact at Colonial Properties, said without hesitation that the Fengs would not be willing to give these to us. In retrospect, it did seem odd that he did not even say, "Let me check, and I'll get back to you." He flat out said the Fengs would not give them to us without even taking the time to ask them. He did say, however, that they would give us certified rent rolls and two years of profit-and-loss (P&L) statements. This may have been acceptable, had they been true. We never did get signed copies of either of these documents from the Fengs. Neither the title company nor our lender required them, which is typically routine procedure of conventional lenders. We later found out that the title officer selected by the Fengs was a partner with the Fengs in their corporation, and she obviously had a vested interest in seeing this transaction close.

If people are telling you the truth in what they report on their financials, they should have nothing to hide and be willing to provide you with the schedule E from their tax return, bank statements, and audited financial statements. If they won't, they have something to hide, and you should run!

TIP 3

Do not enter into an agreement with a seller based exclusively upon his or her own self-generated financial statements, even if they are written in in gold ink.

If the financials are legitimate, the seller should have no problem sharing the source documents of this information with you. Be willing to walk away if things do not add up. We eventually did get the bank statements and the tax returns during the discovery period of our lawsuit, and this included two years of bank statements with no more than $15,000 deposited in any given month. This was quite the contrast to the $28,000 to $30,000 the Fengs had reported to us during the due diligence period. The tax returns matched the bank deposits showing a gross income in 2005 of $150,000 versus the $347,000 that was reported to us.

It is too easy for a seller to pass along bogus information without there being some type of backup documentation. It is okay to accept these seller-created financials when you're first analyzing a property, but never close on a transaction without seeing the source documentation.

TIP 4

Trust your instincts. Don't let the thought of wanting something so much cause you to overlook the obvious warning signs.

During our inspection of the P&L statements, I noticed that the Fengs' financials did not include allowances for utilities, which struck me as odd because the property had only one meter at the street, which meant the electric company was sending one bill to the property, and the tenants were not being billed individually. When I questioned Garrett about it, he had an answer for this as well. He explained to me that the Fengs were billing the tenants for their share of the utilities, and they were not claiming these payments as income, so they did not report the payment they made to the utility companies. To further support his statement, we were sent copies of the utility invoices the Fengs allegedly had issued to their tenants. The explanation seemed to make sense; however, the inconsistencies were beginning to mount.

This should have been a red flag to us at the time. It was something too easily explained away, as it was just the beginning of us discovering the Fengs' poor record keeping and accounting. This was evidenced by the exhibit entitled "The Doodle," which was the financial statement that the Fengs gave Colonial Properties at the time it was given the listing. We wanted this property a little too badly. We were blinded by how impressive everything looked on the surface; we didn't delve deeply enough until it was too late.

Trust your gut.

TIP 5

Do your due diligence. Take nothing for granted.

We were cautiously optimistic about the property but felt we needed more assurance about what we were buying. We hired a local real estate broker, Doyle Hardy of the Ellery James agency, as our would-be property manager to serve as our eyes and ears on the ground during the due diligence and escrow period. The plan was then to have Doyle provide offsite management once we closed on the Crestview. We provided Doyle with the financials we were given by Isaac Davis, and armed with this data and his camera; Doyle visited the property and took almost three-dozen pictures. Doyle agreed with our assessment that the strong financial statements and the freshly painted buildings and manicured grounds made this property attractive to him as well. He gave us his recommendation to move forward based upon the strength of the *fraudulent* financials we were given and the condition of the property at the time of his visit.

As mentioned earlier, Michael did a thorough rent analysis of other C-type properties in Corpus Christi and found that the Crestview Apartments had, in fact, the lowest rents in town with definite potential for increasing the rents to market and yielding even more cash flow. We also contracted with a property-inspection service to go through every single unit and provide us with a list of deferred maintenance, including appliances that would need to be serviced or replaced. We then received quotes on all the deferred maintenance and fixtures, and even after all of these expenses, we still calculated a net profit each year of $60,000.

Pay attention to every detail in order insure that all the information you've been given is accurate. Once you close on a transaction, it is closed and is now your problem.

TIP 6

If the property appears to be a cash-flowing machine, lenders should be lining up to loan you money. If they aren't, you should find out why.

The next issue we ran into was financing. In spite of how good this property looked on paper, we could not get any lender to consider a loan. When we were near the end of our contingency period, Garrett introduced us to Allan Ward of Investors Capital, which was a mortgage broker with its own in-house lending department. After reviewing the financials, Allan said he would lend to us. In fact, the property looked so good that he would even increase the loan to help us take care of some of the deferred maintenance that the property needed. We were now set.

Or so we thought.

Investors started the usual process of requesting all of our financials (tax returns, bank statements, balances in our brokerage accounts, etc.), which we expected. We quickly turned over all the required documents to them. The odd part of this equation was that they did not ask for anything from the Fengs except the Fengs' self-generated financial statements, which we later learned were bogus. The financials the lender accepted weren't from the Fengs at all but were, in fact, created on Garrett's and Isaac's computers. Investors did not ask the Fengs to even sign or authenticate any of these documents. They did, however, ask Michael and me to do so.

We thought this rather bizarre, as typically a lender will require the seller to sign and certify the profit-and-loss statements and rent rolls given to the buyer, acknowledging that this information was true and accurate. We relied upon these documents that were given to us when we made our decision to move forward with the purchase of this property. The lender, who was referred to us by Garrett as well as the escrow agent and Feng business partner May Nguyen, failed to require and enforce this part of our agreement.

Banks are in the business of lending money on good investments. If they won't lend to you, there is something wrong. Find out why!

TIP 7

The sellers' agents have no fiduciary responsibility to you, but they do have a duty not to break the law and commit fraud.

While legally Garrett and Isaac were the Fengs' agents and had no fiduciary duty to us in the sale of the Crestview, they did have a responsibility to not break the law and to pass on information that they knew or should have known was false. We trusted that the code of ethics that bound the agents and the reputation of Colonial Properties as the largest seller of apartment buildings in the country would not allow them to do anything remotely illegal. We were wrong. We assumed we would be treated with the same amount of respect that we afforded to others. When we sold our property in Reno, we disclosed to our buyers that we had held it as a speculative venture, and it had lost money every month. This was the right thing to do. We never considered lying to close the deal. Our integrity was more important to us than any amount of money. If we could not sell our properly honestly, we weren't going to sell it, period.

The fact that the P&Ls and rent rolls were in some form generated on the agents' computers could have been a warning to us. The fact that Garrett and Isaac knew that the Fengs did not keep rent rolls from one month to the next and only kept track of their rent rolls on a piece of binder paper that was thrown away after each month should have been enough evidence to them that the information they were given by the Fengs was inaccurate, if not completely fabricated. The fact that the agents felt it necessary to help the Fengs recreate their rent rolls and financial statements in Excel format, in this case, seemed like an obvious attempt to keep the handwritten chicken scratched versions the Fengs kept, away from any interested parties. Had any buyers, lenders or appraisers actually seen the Feng's shoddy record keeping it certainly would have given them cause for concern about the validity of the information they were being given.

While the sellers' agents do not have a fiduciary responsibility to the buyer, they do have a statutory obligation to not break the law. Passing along documents that the agents knew or should have known were false and that the buyer would rely upon to make the decision to purchase a property is fraud. Always insist on seeing the source documents used to create the financials you've been given!!

TIP 8

The banks do not owe you anything either! It's their job to lend you money; after all, that is why you came to them, right?

We also did not think that the lenders would risk getting this property back by accepting potentially bogus financials. They would have wanted to protect their investment, wouldn't they?

As we later found out, Investors cared very little about the solvency of the property and were more concerned about Michael and me being able to service the debt. This was, at least for a short period of time while they attempted to package our loan with a bunch of other bad paper and then sell them to an unsuspecting bank that was protected by the FDIC. This is exactly what they did. In less than sixty days after we closed on the Crestview, Investors sold our note to Texas Savings and Loan Mortgage, which later did the same thing and sold our loan to FNMA, better known as "Fannie Mae." Because Investors was an in-house lender using its own money to finance the Crestview Apartments, it was not required to be federally insured as were most conventional banks. Texas Savings and Loan did not use its own funds and neither did FNMA, so they were federally regulated and insured. What this meant to Michael and me was that we had none of the protection against mortgage fraud that would have been afforded to us had we borrowed directly from either Texas Savings and Loan or FNMA. We had none of the protection and all of the exposure financially. As Texas was a "recourse" state, we would soon find out that we could not only lose the property, which we ultimately did, but we could lose everything we owned due to the personal guarantee we signed with Investors.

You will find that the bank will be your best friend when you're trying to purchase a property but your worst enemy if you fail to pay. The bank doesn't care if you're defrauded. The bank doesn't care if you've run out of funds. Bankers don't care about your circumstances.

They just want their money!

TIP 9

If you don't feel right, you do not have to close.

The downside of closing on a bad deal is greater than the potential loss you could incur by becoming the owner of a "dog." Besides, if the seller has falsified information in an effort to lure you into the transaction, he or she could be liable for the losses you incur by failing on your 1031 exchange. I remember reading some time ago that when you invest in the stock market you can only lose what you invested. What Michael and I would soon learn was that you could not only make money in real estate but that, without careful scrutiny, you could lose a lot more than your initial investment.

Well, needless to say, because of our high credit scores, income, and savings, we were approved in short order and were set to close on the morning of April 17, 2007. When the day started, we were excited. The due diligence period had been taxing. We were constantly doing either physical evaluations of the property, including inspections, soliciting bids from contractors for the deferred maintenance, and interviewing onsite managers. Not to mention, Investors was putting us through the wringer in order to ensure our ability to repay the loan was sound. It was all exhausting. We were done. We were ready to get down to the business of running the property.

The protocol at a closing is for the seller to provide the buyer with the final rent roll, and then the title company assigns the proration's meaning that, since we were closing midmonth, part of the rents collected would be due to us at the signing. What came next we did not expect.

We were sent the Fengs' final rent roll from Colonial Properties. What we were given was a rent roll that showed over $17,000 of uncollected rent out of $33,000 of potential rent halfway through the month. As it was the seventeenth of the month, all of the uncollected rents were now late. You could have knocked us over with a feather. Nowhere during the previous six months of rent rolls did any of the Fengs' documents show more than $2,500 of uncollected rent. Now we were receiving a rent roll showing uncollected rents over five times what we had been given over any preceding month.

The first thing I did was to call Allan Ward at Investors and ask him to hold the closing until we were given an explanation and a chance to have the Fengs bring the rest of the tenants current. We, of course, felt that the bank would side with us as our loan was secured by the performance of the property, or so we thought.

The next thing I knew, I receive a call from Garrett Brewer, the Fengs' agent, in which he stated that everything was in place to close this loan and that if we did not follow through with the transaction, the Fengs intended to keep our $25,000 in earnest money. He also reminded us that if we did not close, the time on our 1031 tax deferred exchange would lapse and as a result we'd be liable for taxes on nearly $500,000 on the sale of our property in Reno, the proceeds of which we were using to buy Crestview.

The first thing I thought was, *Allan Ward from Investors is our lender and works for us, didn't he? Why did he call Garrett Brewer?* Garrett was the sellers' agent not ours. Why wasn't Allan concerned about all the uncollected rent? Wasn't his note secured by the property? Why would he not be concerned about the uncollected rent?

With our backs against the wall and only days away from being liable for taxes on the $500,000 we made on the sale of the property in Reno as well as the risk of losing our $25,000 in earnest money, we felt we had no choice but to proceed with the closing. We thought that maybe the Fengs had just become lazy in their last month of ownership and were only concerned about collecting their portion of the half month of prorations and would leave it up to us to collect our half. Our attitude was that if the property had been performing for two solid years, there was no reason it would not continue. Little did we know at the time that it had never been producing!

Up until you put your name on the dotted line, you control the situation. You cannot be forced to close if anything is amiss.

TIP 10

Beware of move-in specials.

During our due diligence period, we hired Pedro Mendoza to be our onsite manager to work under Doyle Hardy as the onsite manager. On the morning of April 17, Pedro met Daniel Feng at the property. Without a walk-through of the premises, a transfer of paperwork, or a debriefing of any issues with the Crestview, Daniel flipped the keys to the building to Pedro and left. There was no walk-through, no files exchanged and no briefing. All we had to go with was the April 17 rent roll that had been sent to me by Garrett Brewer. This rent roll showed fifty-eight occupied units. Thus the nightmare began.

Pedro spent the next forty-five days chasing the tenants for the $17,000 of unpaid rent. Some tenants could not pay, so it was necessary to file evictions. Some skipped out in the middle of the night, and some never answered their doors. For those supposedly occupied units in which no one ever responded to Pedro, we did a twenty-four hour notice of entry, and we found many of these units were empty and for who knows how long.

By the first week of June, we were down thirteen units from the original fifty-eight the Fengs had reported as occupied. Forty-five occupied units was our breakeven point. This was the minimum number of occupied units we needed to cover the mortgage, utilities, and management. We were now spending our money taking care of the deferred maintenance, money that was supposed to have come out of the cash flow of the property.

We began running $199 move-in specials in an effort to remedy the vacancy situation. This strategy proved to have some initial success at least for the first month. The second month many of the tenants could not come up with the full rent, so we had to start the eviction process on them, and while we were waiting for our day in court, these vagrant tenants were trashing our units. By the time we were able to get them off the property, the units each required several hundred dollars in repairs, which could have taken Pedro up to a month to complete and re-rent.

We learned the hard way about running move-in specials. They were great for getting someone in the units who could only afford the reduced first month rent. By the second month, most could not pay, and then we were stuck with a tenant we had to evict. The eviction cost more than we received for the first month in terms of filing fees. We also lost revenue due to the unit being occupied while we tried to remove the tenants. While we were trying to evict the tenants, the tenants were damaging their apartments because they were bitter about getting evicted.

Rather than going through the revolving door of tenants and evictions and the costs associated with the move-in specials, you should spend this same money increasing the appeal of your units and charging top dollar to qualified tenants who will appreciate the improvements and stay with you a long time.

TIP 11

**Avoid properties with Master Meters.
This is particularly true if you are going
to try to bill tenants for their portion of
the utilities. The usage of the utilities
is very difficult to apportion evenly.**

We also never came close to covering the utility charges we were being billed by the power company. The water bill was also underreported, as the sewer charges we thought had been part of the water bill were conspicuously omitted from the Fengs' financial statements. When you added the sewer charges to the water bill, this amounted to nearly double what had been reported by the Fengs. Michael and I were now covering the deficit of the 30 percent vacancy, the negative on the water and electric bills, and the turnover costs of the revolving door of tenants to the tune of $10,000 to $15,000 per month.

There is no incentive for tenants who don't have to pay for electricity to control the usage of electricity that you pay for.

TIP 12

Interview the tenants who live in the building for which you are considering to purchase.

You will never know what you'll find out about the owner, the property, or the other tenants if you don't interview some of the people you see on the property while you're making your decision to purchase.

We found that out when we had a pipe break outside the back of the 700 building, which we also discovered was not the first time this had happened. In fact, during the previous ownership the entire bottom floor of the building had been flooded. We had to hire a plumbing contractor to remediate the situation, which required digging up the driveway and replacing pipes. Tenants on the bottom floor had to be relocated to other units; carpets and drywall needed to be replaced to the tune of another $10,000. During the short time in which the Fengs owned this property, the sewer line to this same building had backed up and flooded at least once before. The cost to repair these damages never did appear anywhere on the Fengs' profit and loss statement. In retrospect, one of our biggest mistakes was to have not been present when the inspector went into every unit. This would have been the perfect opportunity to casually interview the tenants.

No one will know the history of your prospective property better than the people that live there. Interview them.

TIP 13

Find out if the local appraisal district offers a property tax protest process for buildings that are underperforming. If it does, open a public records request for the financials that were used to protest these taxes.

By May 2008, we'd had enough. We'd lost nearly $200,000 in operating costs and more than likely our entire $250,000 down payment on the property. We were desperate and a stone's throw of defaulting on the loan. In a moment of desperation, I called Garrett Brewer. At the time, I did not suspect either he or Isaac of any foul play, and as he was familiar with the Crestview Apartments, we hoped he would be able to help us unload it. Garrett, while trying to get us into the property, had always been personable, friendly, and extremely accommodating. This time Michael and I were at wit's end. My credit cards were maxed out, my retirement savings were gone, and Michael's savings were dwindling, and his line of credit on the house he had owned free and clear when this all started was now completely exhausted.

I poured my heart out to Garrett (he later told the jury I was crying, and while this was not true, I certainly felt like it!). I told Garrett we were at the end of our ropes and needed to cut our losses before we went bankrupt. We needed to sell the Crestview. I told him that we had not even been able to recoup the utility expenses that were being charged by the power company. These were the same charges Garrett reported to us that his clients, the Fengs, had been collecting consistently month after month. I was thinking that I would get some sort of shock, awe, sympathy, or even empathy. What I did get from Garrett was something I did not expect. Without hesitation he simply said, "Eh, they (the Fengs) probably lied."

What? Did I hear him correctly? How could Brewer, who along with his co-agent Isaac Davis, who had represented the Fengs for nearly a year, believe that their clients were capable of lying? It was not just a little lie, like fudging a name or two on the rent roll, but one so horrific that it put two unsuspecting buyers, us, on the verge of financial ruin. They lied? The Fengs probably lied about collecting the money from their tenants for their utility bills? Michael and I counted on these funds as part of the financial analysis when we were making our decision to purchase Crestview. How could they have lied to us? This false information was what we relied on to seek nearly $1.5 million in financing, which was backed by the performance of the property. It was based on this false information that we signed a personal guarantee that was backed by our personal assets and the homes in which our families lived. If they lied about this fact, what else could they have lied about? As I stated in the beginning of this book, Garrett later denied saying that the Fengs lied, and he said that I said they lied. I am not sure how I would have known if the Fengs lied, since I only dealt with Colonial Properties and did not even know the Fengs. Regardless of which you care to believe, it was that phone call that initiated the largest manhunt conducted by two laymen investors that ever hit the real estate industry.

I couldn't help but guess that Garrett felt a little satisfaction in the fact that we were so damaged by this sale. After all, Michael and I had put the Fengs through the ringer collecting six months of rent rolls, requesting all sorts of financial data including tax returns, bank statements, and utility bills, and having the gall to hire an inspector to go through every single one of the units at Crestview. Furthermore, when the inspections were done and quotations were submitted for the work, we had the nerve to ask for a credit back from the Fengs! A credit that Garrett, we suspect, never requested of the Fengs. How dare we try to get a fair and accurate picture of how this property (and his clients) had been performing!

One thing I have learned from being in business for myself for twenty-five years is not to say or do anything that would allow my emotions to get in the way. I wanted to think about this statement regarding the Fengs "lying" a little further though, after the call, so I proceeded to ask Garrett what price he could get for the building.

The first thing he asked me was for a copy of our rent roll and a financial statement, and then he would analyze it and get back to me with the amount for which he could list it. A few days passed, and Garrett called. The news was not shocking when he told us he could not even sell the Crestview for what we owed on the property. He did tell me, "If you fill it up, I could sell it. Buyers will buy on a trend." This was another "aha" moment for us. Is it possible that he and Isaac had this conversation with the Fengs several months earlier?

It was as though the fog had cleared. For a year, I wondered about how these two Chinese immigrants who barely spoke English and did not even know how to use a computer were capable of grossing $350,000 a year on a shoestring budget while Michael and I invested $80,000 in improvements and were hardly able to scratch out $200,000? This was nearly a $150,000 swing. All of a sudden, we no longer trusted anything we had been told about the Crestview Apartments.

It was about this time that I received a solicitation from Samuel Mayer of Property Tax Negotiators offering its services to help us protest the new assessment we received from the Nueces County Appraisal District. The assessment we received in 2008 had increased the value of the Crestview by nearly $600,000 over the year before even though we'd lost tens of thousands of dollars. Property Tax Negotiators would use our financial statements as well as other data to explain to the Nueces County Appraisal Board why the increased valuation was not justified. Property Tax Negotiators' fee would be based on a percentage of what it was able to save us in property taxes. We figured that with our sad state of affairs this would be a slam dunk. It never occurred to me when we bought Crestview that the property taxes in Texas were determined differently than they were in California, where we had Proposition 13. Prop. 13 is a statute in which the tax basis of real estate is based upon the original purchase price of the property.

In California, where we lived, the tax basis was based upon the actual purchase price, and the values were frozen at the purchase price with only a small allowance made for increases in value each year. In Texas, things were different. The governing board of the appraisal district had the discretion to increase the value of every property in its jurisdiction every year, and it was then incumbent on the property owner to hire someone such as Property Tax Negotiators to protest the increase and, hopefully, to get the taxes reduced on the property. The increased amount of our taxes without the protest would cost us an additional $16,000 per year. What did we have to lose? I asked Samuel Mayer, the owner of the company, how he came across our name, and he informed me that he had protested the Fengs' property taxes the year before. So I nonchalantly inquired as to how successful he'd been working for the Fengs. He informed me that the original assessment of the Crestview in 2005 was $1,550,000, and, through his efforts, he was able to get the value of the Crestview reduced to $950,000. This was only a slight increase over the $850,000 the Fengs had been assessed two years earlier.

At this point, I asked if Mayer would send me the financials he had used to protest the Fengs' taxes the year before. While I really did not expect he'd send it, I felt I had to ask. In minutes, the fax was coming through on my machine with a one-page profit and loss statement from the Fengs. The Fengs' P&L, to my surprise, showed a $24,000 loss against $147,000 collected rent! This profit and loss statement was a huge departure from the $350,000 in gross revenue and $200,000 in profit the Fengs had told us they made. The Fengs had used Property Tax Negotiators and this financial statement to get the assessed value of the Crestview Apartments reduced $600,000! The Fengs had lied. They either lied to us or to the Nueces County Appraisal District. Judging by our $200,000 in losses, I think we know to whom they lied. It seemed apparent that the Fengs had freely lied to whomever they wished in order to get what they wanted. We were now on a mission to gather more evidence to implicate them in this case of fraudulent misrepresentation.

The appraisal district may not be the only entity which may have copies of your property's financial history that are public record. Check with both the local city and county government to see if there may be another branch that does. Don't forget to check with the assessor's office!

TIP 14

Seek out the name of the former owner and the title company that handled the transaction.

If you can contact the prior owner of your property to make sure that the information you were given by the seller is commensurate with what the owner sold to them. This could be particularly valuable if the current seller only had the property for a short period of time. Through our research of the tax rolls and county recorder, we learned that the Fengs had acquired the Crestview from Janie Sinclair in October 2004. We inquired of one of the older tenants, and fortunately that person had Janie's phone number. Janie lived in San Bernadino, only about forty-five minutes from us. I called her and found her very accommodating, and she agreed to send us her final profit and loss statement and rent roll that was generated by her office just prior to turning over the property to the Fengs. Needless to say, when the Fengs took over the property in October 2004, the occupancy was a mere 30 percent.

You should request a rent roll from your seller from their first month of ownership to verify that the occupancy at the time they purchased the property was the same as what they reported to you as their as their starting occupancy level. You can also verify what they tell you with the selling agent, the assessor's office, the appraisers office or the title company that handled the transaction.

These figures should be fairly close if not exact. If they are not, you need to ask why. You should also compare the occupancy of the property from the first month your seller purchased the property to the most recent month the seller reported the occupancy to you. If the occupancy jumped significantly, you should ask why.

TIP 15

Find out if the water department offers credits for vacant units.

Michael and I learned during our brief tenure as the owners of the complex that the City of Corpus Christi Water Department allowed for a small credit each month to owners whose buildings were not completely full. In the event that owners such as the Fengs wanted a credit on their water bill, they would have to file a report with the city each month they wanted a credit and list all the vacant units. The Water Department in turn would issue a small credit for the sewer portion of the bill for each vacancy. This would be done under the assumption that vacant units did not create wastewater back into the sewer system. We suspected that the opportunistic Fengs would not want to miss any opportunity to save money, so we did an open record request for any vacancy reports filed on the property during the Fengs' tenure.

Our suspicions were correct. The Fengs filed a report virtually every month they owned the property. The reports showed that for twenty-four solid months, from the time the Fengs purchased the Crestview, the property had no more than 45 percent occupancy, and most of the time it hovered around 33 percent occupancy.

The reports we received from the Water Department showed no change in occupancy all the way through 2006. In July 2006, when the Fengs engaged Brewer and Davis for a property listing, Crestview was still reported by the Fengs as less than 50 percent occupied. The agents would later provide us with a profit and loss statement for this month showing that the building was 95 percent occupied.

We were on a mission. We knew there were more people that had first-hand experience of the property. As we had been visited regularly by city inspectors, we knew that they too had to keep records that were available to us.

You can also request an open records request from the utility departments for the usage on the property. If the owner reports that the occupancy has gone up significantly over several months, but the utility usage has not changed, this could be worthy of further investigation.

TIP 16

Contact city officials, including code enforcement, fire inspectors, and the Health Department. You never know what you will find!

We then called code enforcement and requested an open records report for any citations that may have been issued to the Fengs during the period of time in which they had the Crestview on the market. We were not surprised to find that on November 8, 2006, code enforcement Officer Jim Starr visited Crestview and cited the Fengs for "rubbish and abandoned vehicles." Five days later, on November 13, he returned and issued another citation to the Fengs for multiple abandoned vehicles and more trash on the property.

The irony was that this most recent citation was written one day before Isaac Davis sent me this e-mail with respect to the Crestview Apartments:

> "Jack,
>
> I've attached a marketing flyer on the best two cash-flowing properties I'm currently selling. Both are C-class deals and both are decent shape and in good locations.
> Please let me know should you have further questions.
>
> Thanks,
> Isaac Davis
> Senior Advisor
> Colonial Properties"

Government officials are the easiest witnesses to find. After all, they are government officials. They are required to write reports, they have offices, and they are in the public sector. Look for them; they are there.

TIP 17

Insist on prior year tax returns, bank statements, or audited financials, or, better yet, all three!

As we went through a forensic analysis of the material we were given by Colonial and through the open records reports from our lawsuit we found it interesting that Brewer and Davis who had signed a six-month listing agreement with the Fengs in July of 2006 waited until the end of August before they started to market the property. Why would they let two months of a six-month agreement lapse before they listed it? Were they just lazy or could they have known that they could not sell the Crestview for the price that the Fengs wanted considering the condition it was in without some improvements to the exterior of the property?

Do you think that the agents felt that it would have been difficult to convince buyers that the property was running 95% occupancy as the rent rolls indicated considering the 50% level Jane admitted to having in July 2006? Could they not see the obvious farce that the Fengs were trying to perpetrate in telling the public their building was at near capacity when it was barely half full?

Presuming the Feng's had duped the agents as Davis and Brewer claimed they did didn't it strike them as funny that two people who were anxious to sell their building for top dollar would not have a financial statement or a rent roll to give them for over five weeks into their six month listing agreement?

How was it they could not get financials from the Fengs until August 2006 and yet when they finally did their profit and loss statements dated all the way back to January 2005? Didn't this raise a red flag that these documents may have been contrived?

How did they settle on a listing price in July without getting the financials from which the asking price typically would have been determined until August?

As the months passed, Michael and I did our own forensic analysis of this transaction. It now became apparent to us that the statement that Garrett made indicating that the Fengs 'did not report their utility expenses because they allegedly billed the tenants for power and therefore did not report the income', never did, in fact, come from the Fengs. Garrett never said, "Let me check." He came up with this response on the spot without even taking time to even pretend he inquired of the Fengs about why these figures did not appear on the P&L. He answered the question himself, without calling the Fengs. In fact, come to think of it, we doubt very much that he ever asked the Fengs for their bank statements or the tax returns as we had requested. He just told me they would not give them to us. Was Garrett afraid that the Fengs might have given us their returns and thereby alerting us that the financials which we were given were contrived?

When we asked for a credit on the deferred maintenance from the Fengs, Garrett never even pretended to ask them. He just told us they would not give us a credit. Were Garrett and Isaac overstepping their bounds as the Fengs agents by answering questions for their clients that they never asked of them? Would the Feng's have been willing to give us a credit? Were the agents afraid that a lower sales price to us would have meant less commissions to them? Of course it would.

We felt that at this point we had the goods on the Fengs but wanted to make sure that they had something worth going after. They had walked away from our closing table with $997,000, part of which was our money, but most if belonged to the bank for which we had signed a personal guarantee.

It was less than eighteen months since we had closed on Crestview. They couldn't have squandered all our money that quickly, could they? We hired a private investigator to do an asset search on the Fengs. They made nearly $1 million on the transaction. We needed to know where it was if we had any hope of recovering our losses in court. We conducted a nationwide search of bank accounts, brokerage, and retirement accounts, and to our disappointment we found they had no more than $1,600 in any one bank account. Where did the money go?

We felt that we'd gone as far as we could without filing a lawsuit against the Fengs. We knew in our hearts that Davis and Brewer shared some responsibility for what had happened to us, but we needed the Fengs' testimony to get a judgment on them. We did feel there was not any more information we would be privy to in the public sector without initiating a lawsuit. This was where things became worse for us, rather than better. Now, in addition to covering the negative cash flow on the building, we had to start covering the legal fees, which in some months exceeded the deficit on the property. We were leaking oil pretty bad. We communicated monthly with the bank, covering our mortgage payments and the bills out of our dwindling credit to keep the property solvent. At one point, the vice president with whom I was working told me, "In forty years of banking, I have never encountered such stand-up guys as you and Michael."

In spite of the Fengs not having any appreciable assets, we felt we had no alternative but to file a lawsuit against them, as we could not get to Garrett and Isaac and their errors and omission insurance without first filing suit on Daniel and June. Yet, we still wanted to know where our money went. We even went to the title company and requested a copy of the check the Fengs were given at closing, and by looking at the back of the canceled check, we were able to determine where it had been deposited. We then filed a subpoena for the banking information from Corpus City Bank, the bank that we suspected the Fengs had used to launder the money they received from the sale of Crestview.

What we found is that Daniel and June opened the account three days before our closing, and by the fourth day after this check was deposited in their account, the money was gone. We traced the disbursements and found they had purchased multiple certificates of deposit for $100,000 each and made one large withdrawal for $400,000. When the CDs matured in ninety days, they split up the proceeds and bought several more CDs. At this point Eve Schlouter, the attorney for the Fengs, caught wind of what we were doing and filed a motion for us to cease our investigation on the grounds that what we were doing constituted post-judgment discovery or otherwise information to which we were not entitled to until we had a judgment.

While we were discouraged that the Fengs didn't have money just sitting in a bank account waiting for us to come collect it, we still felt we had a case against Davis and Brewer. The circumstantial evidence made it difficult to believe the agents at the very least didn't know what was going on, and in the grander scheme had a hand in helping to make the Fengs' story believable. They were showing units and bringing by prospective buyers, and spent a considerable amount of time helping the Fengs assemble the financials that would be given to potential buyers. These were seasoned agents who later admitted under oath at trial that they routinely evaluated nearly two hundred properties a year. How could the Fengs have hidden nearly forty vacant units from them for six months?

We knew that the Fengs had worked with Isaac Davis two years earlier to sell the Casa Blanca Apartments, which was another "C" property also located in Corpus Christi, so we thought it might be interesting to obtain information on the history of this transaction. We discovered that it was almost a carbon copy of our transaction. The building was listed at 95 percent occupancy and sold to an out-of-state buyer. The buyer invested $200,000 improving the property and then escaped by the skin of his teeth when he sold the property eleven months later for significantly less than the purchase price with only 65 percent occupancy.

When we pulled the water reports for this property, we were not surprised to find that the Fengs reported only 45 percent occupancy for the entire period of time they owned Casa Blanca.

What we also later learned was that the Fengs did not use the 1031 exchange process, a method to defer the taxes on the gain from the proceeds they earned on Casa Blanca to purchase Crestview. This meant that the Fengs were liable for taxes of $250,000 on the profit of $800,000 they had earned on the sale of the Casa Blanca Apartments. This also struck us as odd considering how the Fengs took advantage of every loophole they could. It made no sense that they would not use a 1031 exchange and would pay a quarter million dollars in taxes, considering they bought Crestview a mere two months after they sold Casa Blanca Apartments and could have saved $250,000 had they "rolled" their gain over to purchase the Crestview. We later found out why they did not take advantage of the 1031 exchange. The Fengs were not in this alone, and more than likely their other investors wanted to be paid.

It wasn't long after we filed suit on the Fengs that we were contacted by Eve Schlouter, the Fengs' lawyer, with an offer to settle. The Fengs, who apparently felt we had a significant amount of damaging evidence against them, offered to take the Crestview back from us and take over the loan. They made no offer to reimburse us for our down payment or the loss of cash we realized by holding this white elephant. We felt, considering the losses we were surmounting, we needed to consider this offer. We hoped they would cooperate in court if they were off the hook and be honest about exactly what the agents knew, including but not limited to, how their financials were created, the true occupancy of the property, and other details surrounding the sale of the Crestview Apartments. Unfortunately for us, we had communicated so effectively with the bank regarding the fraud that had been perpetrated upon us that Texas Savings and Loan wanted no part of the Fengs. As the note holder, the bank rejected the Fengs' offer, as its officers felt more secure with Michael and me on the hook than they did the Fengs, who appeared to have no appreciable assets to back up the loan.

There was another contingency on the offer from Daniel and June. The Fengs had the audacity to stipulate that if they were to take the property back and that if for some reason Colonial Properties sued them for involving them in the lawsuit, we would have to defend them! It was based upon this request that we surmised that the Fengs had incriminating evidence on Isaac and Garrett, and they were scared to death they'd be released from our lawsuit only to find themselves in another lawsuit with Colonial Properties. This fear seemed to permeate the entire civil process, as we would later find out, because in spite of the Fengs being released from the lawsuit, they never admitted anything that would incriminate Davis and Brewer.

We knew that if we were to prevail, we needed to get the agents, who were insured by Colonial Properties' errors and omissions policy, included in the lawsuit. Michael and I were convinced that the agents knew the information they had provided to us from Daniel and June was false if, in fact, they hadn't actually help create it themselves. We also knew that the only ones who could testify to this fact were the Fengs.

Most people won't want to give you their entire tax return; however, investors understand that a buyer will want to see the Schedule E of their tax return, as this portion of their filing should virtually contain all the information on the profit and loss statement that was given. While it is not to say that a seller won't lie to the IRS, it is more likely someone would try to lie to you by giving you a fictitious financial statement. This is certainly one way you can verify what you've been given.

THE DEPOSITIONS

The following excerpts from a series of depositions conducted with Daniel and June Feng, the principal defendants, Garrett Brewer and Isaac Davis the real estate brokers and co-defendants in our lawsuit. We have also included testimony from Sam Wright and Walter Acevedo two Corpus Christi police officers, Juanita Suarez, the former manager of the adjacent apartment complex to the Crestview apartments and Jenna Valdez, a competing real estate agent who visited the property with a perspective client both a month before our visit and a month subsequent to our visit.

The depositions begin with the sellers and the brokers in order to reveal the fraudulent behavior they exhibited during the sale of the Crestview Apartments. We then presented depositions and affidavits from impartial witnesses during the same period in time whom had no interest in the sale of the property. Their testimonies were offered as evidence of the dilapidated condition and haven for crime that was the Crestview Apartments prior to our visits, a property that was ultimately and deceptively sold to us.

We present these depositions as part of the forensic evidence we uncovered during the two years the following the time in which this crime was perpetrated upon us as cautionary signs in an effort to help the reader avoid similar pitfalls.

On June 11, 2009, we deposed both June and Daniel Feng at 9:17 a.m. at the law firm of Schlouter, Andrews, and Jones. We were represented by our attorney, Harlan Peabody, and the Fengs by Harriet Cantor, as Eve Schlouter had another commitment. Debbie Fife, The attorney for Garrett and Isaac also attended the Fengs' depositions. This was the first time since 2006 we'd faced the Fengs.

The interview started off slowly where our attorney, Harlan Peabody, asked a number of formal questions such as June's name, which was actually Ling Feng; her place of birth, which was China; and her education, which was microbiology. June was in graduate school studying molecular biology when she dropped out to start a family. Daniel, on the other hand, was educated as a statistician.

June's demeanor was particularly agitated. She gave off the air that she was nervous but also very indignant that she was being sued and interrogated for a matter in which she felt she'd done no wrong. Daniel was definitely the weakest of the pair, and when it came to any questions regarding materials that we were given, he pleaded ignorance. When asked how the information on the spreadsheets was created, Daniel also confessed that he did not know how to create spreadsheets using Excel. We found this particularly interesting because he was supposedly educated as a statistician.

During the Feng depositions, it was apparent that June Feng wore the pants in the family and did not speak English very well, at least she pretended not to. She used this to her advantage by giving broken answers, acting as though she did not understand Harlan Peabody's questions, and sometimes not answering the questions at all. When she did give a coherent answer, she gave off the air that she was completely justified in giving us false financials. As she put it, "The buyer should buy on what the building could do, not what the building was actually doing." She said at one point.

In some respects, she was right. People do buy on what they think the property will do; however, they should only pay for that property with the knowledge of what it was truly doing. If they wanted to pay more, they should only do so knowing the true financial condition of the building. For instance, a buyer could choose to pay more for a building whose financials did not justify the sale price of the building if the buyer knew that the neighborhood in which the building was located could support higher rents.

June had the attitude that the end justified the means. During each of the depositions, June was shown the financials we were given by Garrett and Isaac. These were financials that she supposedly had created. She appeared to not recognize them. When asked if she created them, she said, "They must have been created from information they provided."

During Mr. Peabody's questioning, he asked June the following:

Q. When you ran the Crestview Apartments, did you keep a rent roll every month?
A. No.

How was it then that we were provided six months of rent rolls?

Peabody then had June identify a rent roll from September 2006 and asked:

Q. Now, is this the kind of a rent roll or a kind—is this the kind of list of your tenants that you described that you were keeping before?

A. No.

Q. Okay. This was a rent roll that you created for the purpose of selling the property. Is that right?

A. Yes.

Q. Okay. How did the list that you kept previously to this Exhibit No. 1 differ?

A. Just the number.

Q. Okay.

A. And the amount of the rent. Then when they pay, put the date, how much they paid, just like that.

Q. Okay. Now, did you keep one of those for each month that you operated the property?

A. Not each month. After the month, update, and the old one, maybe throw it away.

How was it then that we were provided twenty-four months of financial statements if they did not keep monthly records? According to June's testimony, she did not keep any records.

Q. Did the bank require you to provide financial statements concerning the Crestview Apartments on an ongoing basis after they made the loan?

A. Maybe. I don't remember.

Q. Did you send the bank financial statements periodically?

A. They don't ask.

Q. The bank did not require you to send them periodically financial statements about the Crestview Apartments?

A. Maybe once a year.

Q. Did you prepare those?

A. Yes.

Q. Nobody else did?

A. Only me.

Q. Okay. Did you keep copies of those financial statements?

A. No.

Q. Did you keep them for some period of time after you sent them to the bank?

A. No. Just fax over.

Q. So you would fax them over and immediately throw them away?

A. Sometimes I give to them. I go to their office and give to them.

Q. So you would give them the only copy that you had?

A. I don't know if I have any.

When asked about the financial statement Michael and I were given by the agents:

Q. Okay. Did you have a conversation about this financial statement with Mr. Davis?

A. I remember he said that they don't need the bank deposit. They don't need the tax return. They only need this for the loan.

Q. So you were doing this because Mr. Davis told you that the bank would need something for a loan. Is that correct?

A. Yes.

Could it be that Isaac and Garrett did not want us to get the tax returns or the bank statements?

Did they know that once we were given these documents that we'd know the financial statements we were given were false? Theoretically the gross income on the tax returns and the deposits into the Fengs' bank account should all be the same, right? Why would Isaac tell June that neither of these documents would be necessary? Why would he state that only the unverifiable financial statements were required? Wasn't the fact that it took the Fengs two months of the listing agreement to produce a financial statement a red flag? Why would he not say, "Just give me your tax return or what you gave to your CPA to prepare your taxes for last year"?

How did Garrett know how the Fengs allocated their electricity bills when he did not ask them? How did he know the Fengs would not turn over their tax returns or bank statements, when he did not ask them either? How did he know they would not credit us for the deferred maintenance? Why? I think we now knew.

We now felt that the Fengs had accomplices. While the Fengs never "outed" Isaac or Garrett, the agents were more than happy to throw the Fengs under the bus in order to save their own skins.

TIP 18

If it looks like a rat and smells like a rat, it probably is!

Through the electronic signature, we discovered every document we received during due diligence and escrow had, in fact, been created on either Garrett's or Isaac's computers. Any time that June was asked what information she shared with the agents and who prepared the financial statements we were provided, June had a sudden case of amnesia. For instance:

Q. You were interested in selling the Casa Blanca Apartments. What did he ask you for?
A. You mean Crestview Apartments?
Q. Uh-huh.
A. He asked for rent roll.
Q. He wanted a rent roll?
A. Yeah.
Q. Did he want financial statements?
A. Yes.
Q. Did you have those?
A. No.
Q. Did you create them for him?
A. Yes.
Q. Did he help you to create those?
A. From the computer, you mean?
Q. Well, in any way. Tell me what he did.
A. I don't remember.

Q. Did you start from scratch and make your own financial statements for the sale of the Crestview Apartments?

A. Yes.

Q. When you say—you said something earlier about put into the computer. Is that—?

A. I didn't put in computer. I think—I don't remember.

Q. Okay. Did you advise Mr. Davis or anybody else at Colonial Properties that these numbers contained estimates?

A. I don't remember.

Q. Okay. Do you think that your husband would have sent something to Mr. Davis if he had prepared it, if Mr. Davis had, in fact, prepared it?

A. I don't remember. Sometimes the—I don't remember.

Q. (By Ms. Fife) So you don't remember, one way or another, who prepared this?

A. No.

If something sounds too good to be true it probably is!

TIP 19

Inspect the metadata on the financials to see who authored them. If they were done by anyone other than the seller, insist on the source documents that were used to create this document.

June gave a lengthy and confusing description of how she generated her financial statements. She described how she based the income on her financial statement, not on actual numbers but what the rent would be once the apartments were stabilized. She did not recall if she ever discussed this with Isaac.

Q. What did you do to give Mr. Davis financial statements for the Crestview Apartments after he asked when you listed the property with him?

A. When—when he asked for that, we already getting much better, and we know if we sell it—I could sell it. So I do—I did the other—I used the present income. How to say that? You know, the past, I used that to give the past.

Q. I'm not sure I understand what you're saying. I'm sorry. Are you trying to describe to me how you created the financial statements that you gave to Mr. Davis?

A. The numbers. The numbers, I used the present at that time—

Q. Uh-huh.

A. —to make the thing in the past two years.

Q. So did you—

A. Year and a half.

Q. Am I to understand that you—you—for example—well, I don't want to put the words in your mouth. Would you tell me specifically what you did?

A. I used the numbers at the time.

Q. Uh-huh. And what numbers do you mean?

A. Income.

Q. Okay.

A. And created the thing in the past.

Q. So did you go back and create—or did you go back and check your records for past months?

A. No. I just used the numbers from the time he asked, and then I did the past.

Q. So you assumed—

A. Similar, yeah.

As one can see it is very easy for a seller to make up a financial statement. That being the case it is imperative that every seller supplied document should be scrutinized for authenticity. The buyer should take no chances, verify everything!

The author of all documents should be established. If it is an Excel spreadsheet, click on File, then Properties, then Details, or if it is a PDF, the author can be found by going to the Properties tab under the File drop-down. The tax returns should also be signed by the CPA that prepared them.

TIP 20

Interview the seller.

In this case, June did not feel she did anything wrong, and if we had been given an opportunity to discuss how these financials were generated, she probably would have come clean or at the very least given us some serious doubt as to their accuracy. It was obvious that Isaac and Garrett did not want us to meet the Fengs or have any contact with them as we saw evidenced by the whole "they're (the Fengs) unwilling to give us their tax return or bank statement nor credit us for the deferred maintenance" fiasco.

At one point in her deposition, June admitted that Isaac had in fact created the professional-looking financial statements we were given:

Q. Okay. What is that?
A. Financial.
Q. Okay. Is that the same year as the exhibit we just discussed, Exhibit No. 3, 2005? Is that also for 2005?
A. It's the same.
Q. Okay. Did you create the typed version that is contained in Exhibit 4?
A. I don't remember.
Q. So if you didn't do it, who might have?
A. Isaac.
Q. (By Mr. Peabody) Would your husband have done this, Mr. Feng?
A. I think Isaac.
Q. Okay.
A. He helped put together.

As the line of questioning continued, it appeared as though the financials we were given included information that was not part of the Fengs' handwritten version of the financial statement:

Q. Okay. Anticipated my next question. You don't know who did the totals?

A. I don't remember.

Q. Do you remember doing it yourself?

A. Here, I did. That's my handwriting. (Indicating.)

Q. Okay. But do you remember adding to Exhibit No. 4 the columns and the rows that total up the income items?

A. I don't remember.

Q. The expense items?

A. I don't remember.

Everyone paints with a different brush. You can find out a lot about a person's integrity and values by spending a few minutes with him or her.

TIP 21

Ask who created the financial statements and the rent rolls. Compare the names of the tenants in the units from one month to the next for consistency.

Harlan tried to establish the occupancy level of the Crestview Apartments when the Fengs identified the Crestview as their next project. According to June's testimony, the Crestview Apartments had just been hit by a hurricane prior to their purchase:

Q. (By Mr. Peabody) The tornado damaged the roof on all of the buildings, one of the buildings?
A. The major one is Building 7. The whole building is vacant when I go there.
Q. And I'm sorry. The whole building?
A. Vacant.
Q. Okay. So when you purchased it, was Building 7 unable to be used?
A. No. I haven't fixed it yet. I haven't finished the damage yet.

Harlan finally pinned June down that the financial statements that we were given by Isaac (which he aided in preparing) were actually pro forma estimates and not the actual historical data that we were led to believe.

Q. Okay. Do you know that this 2005 profit-and-loss statement was given to my clients in their decision-making process about whether to buy this apartment complex?
A. No. It's for the loan.

Q. Okay. Do you know whether they saw it or not?

A. I don't know. They should. I think they should see it.

Q. Okay. Is there anything on this that indicates that any of these numbers are estimates?

A. Yes.

Q. Well, what?

A. The income. The income.

Q. Okay. Can you tell me, if I look at Exhibit 4, what on here would tell a reader that those numbers for income are estimates?

A. If they know the history of the property, because they hire their real estate agent. The agent knows the owner and the daughter. If you know the history and the tornado, you know this is wrong.

The perfect question we should have asked here would have been "Did your agent's Isaac and Garrett know the history of the property?"

Q. Okay.

A. This is just for the loan.

Q. But you have to know something about the property and the history of the property to know that the numbers on this financial statement are not accurate. Is that correct?

A. Yes.

Please allow me to reiterate. Michael and I were out-of-state buyers and did not have the benefit of knowing the history of Crestview. We even had Doyle Hardy, a local broker, review the financials and inspect every single unit, after which he gave us his recommendation to proceed. The one agent that did know the history of the property was Isaac Davis. He knew the Fengs, having sold other properties for them. He attempted to get the listing for the Crestview from Jane Sinclair in 2004 when the tornado had torn the roof of Building 7.

Michael and I only had the benefit of the appearance of the property at the time we visited and the alleged financials to rely upon, which, in this case, were completely fabricated again, with Isaac's help.

Had we been given the handwritten documents the Fengs gave Isaac, we certainly would not have moved forward without having insisted upon the tax returns and bank statements, which Garrett told us they would not give us.

If someone is just making up information, the more rent rolls and financials you get, the more likely he or she will get sloppy and mix up tenants, unit numbers, deposit amounts, or some other pertinent information. The total collected on the rent roll should equal the income on the profit and loss statement. Checks and balances, don't overlook them!

TIP 22

Get to know the history of the property.

This tip comes straight from June Feng. Interview the tenants, the neighbors, the agent who represented the seller, the mailman, and the cable guy. If you are an out-of-state buyer, you can rely upon others who know the "history" of the property. When asked about the difference between the financials that we were given and the ones June used to protest her 2006 property taxes, here's how the line of questioning went and her responses:

Harlan went on to review the profit and loss statement in Exhibit No. 4 which showed that the Crestview Apartments had net operating income of $264,548 which Jane confirmed.

He went on to question the validity of this statement.

Q. But that is not actually what the Crestview Apartments earned in 2005. Is that correct?

A. Yes. Yes.

Q. That is correct?

A. Yes.

Q. But there's no way of knowing when you look at Exhibit No. 4 that that isn't the actual income of the property. Is that correct?

A. Yes.

Q. Now, you told me, I think, earlier that the—well, let me ask you a couple more questions about the 2005 statement used to protest your taxes. Can you describe to me the reason that you created this financial statement? You said protest taxes. Tell me what means, please.

A. The—every year, they increase the property tax, the appraisal. And you take pictures. You have to give something to the one you hire. They go there to do the protest.

Q. Okay.

A. They told me they needed this, so I make this, too.

Q. So you were seeking to have your property tax appraisal lowered, so that you would pay less property taxes to Nueces County and the school district in Corpus Christi. Is that correct?

A. Yes.

Q. And you knew it was important that that financial statement be accurate. Correct?

A. Yes.

Q. And this Exhibit No. 5 is accurate. Is that correct?

A. About right. I don't—maybe not exactly right, but ...

Q. But very close?

A. Yes.

Q. Okay. And Exhibit No. 4 is not correct. It does not actually reflect what income was earned, both on a gross basis and on a net basis for 2005. Correct?

A. I told you this is—I did a retrospect.

Q. "Retrospective"—

A. Yeah.

Q. —is that the word you're looking for?

A. Yes, yes.

Q. And I don't mean to put words in your mouth, but—okay. But, again, nothing that shows that this is retrospective. Correct?

A. Yes.

Harlan continues to question Jane on the comparison of the income statement she gave to us and her tax returns and then to her bank statements and again it was the same response. She felt fully justified in giving us a pro forma income statement and passing it off as the actual income the Crestview was actually producing. When backed into a corner she consistently claimed amnesia.

You won't have to dig too far to find someone, in our case it was Property Tax Negotiators, who knows what your target property was doing before you entered the picture. Get the facts!

TIP 23

Never, ever close on a property exclusively on a seller's financial statements alone!

Harlan continued his examination of Jane and her fabricated financials and the fact that she represented the property was netting over 10 times the amount of income it truly was.

At this point, Harlan compares the 2006 profit and loss statement in which the Feng's claimed to earn $264,000 yet reported to the IRS and the Nueces County appraisal district they'd lost $24,000. The difference between these two financial statements equated to a $250,000 swing.

The Feng's were obviously lying to someone and I think we know who it was and why we went $200,000 in the red our first year in ownership of the Crestview Apartments.

Harlan concluded this line of questioning of June with the following:

Q. If you were buying a piece of property that you thought had earned $264,000 but actually knew that it had earned a loss of $24,000, would that affect your decision to buy the property?

A. (No response.)

Q. Would that be important to you to know in making a decision about whether to buy?

A. Not much.

Q. (By Mr. Peabody) Okay.

A. Minor.

Mrs. Feng would later to testify that it was essentially the buyers responsibility to verify the information they were given or in the Feng's case to catch them in their lie.

If the financials on the property are legitimate, there will be verifiable information to corroborate the information the seller has given you such as tax returns, bank statements, etc.

TIP 24

Don't accept anything at face value.

The fact that June felt it was okay to buy an underperforming property at top dollar was not evident by the financials we were given. If Mrs. Feng truly believed the financial performance of her property was not important, she would have given us the actual financials, which showed that the property had been losing money the entire time she and Daniel owned it.

We had nothing other than the financials we were given and the appearance of the property by which to make our decision. We were kept at arm's length from the Fengs. If we had an opportunity to visit with June and Daniel, it would have been clearly evident that they did not value integrity by the same yardstick as Michael and I. The fact that this property was screaming cash flow on paper but did not sell in the first week and was still on the market six months later spoke volumes.

At this point in the deposition, June attempted to convince Harlan that they had collected much more than their $147,000 for 2005 than her bank deposits reflected. She wanted those present at the deposition to believe that they were skimming more than 25 percent of the cash from their collections before making a deposit in the bank. This could only be believed however, if the rents they were receiving were all cash, as they could not skim checks, money orders, Section 8 payments or cashier's checks. Anyone in the apartment business would find it hard to believe that a sixty-six-unit complex in a blue-collar neighborhood would accept this much cash, as it would be highly irregular. The risk of theft or loss with cash would make it virtually irreplaceable.

Harlan continued with his questioning of June Feng.

Q. Well, I'm asking about, in general. You said sometimes that you would spend money before—you would spend rent collections before you put them in the bank?

A. Yes.

Q. And that that varied every month?

A. Yes.

Q. And what I'm trying to understand is: What is the general range of the percentage of rents collected that you might spend on expenses before you deposited them in the bank?

A. I don't remember. Different every month.

Q. Okay. And, again, I asked you if it might be as much as 25 percent in any given month, and you said sometimes it might be more than that.

A. Yes.

Q. Is that right?

A. Yes.

Q. Would it be as much as half?

A. I don't know. Every month we have some cash and spending.

Q. Uh-huh. Let me ask you this question: Did you keep records of cash expenditures made each month at the Crestview Apartments?

A. We estimate our living expenses.

Q. Okay. But did you keep any records of cash expenditures—

A. No.

Q. —paid?

A. No.

Don't be afraid to ask questions. Don't assume the seller is being honest. In retrospect, we gave too much of the benefit of the doubt to the Fengs. The monthly income reported on the rent rolls from them did not equal the income reported on the P&L. It was close but should have been exact. The tenants' names on the rent roll moved from one unit to the next and then back again the following month. Sometimes this happens due to a water leak or some other work that needed to be done in the original unit, but you should never assume it.

TIP 25

Ask to see an itemized spreadsheet of expenses in the same way that you get a person-by-person accounting of income through the rent roll.

The worst-case scenario is that you have to ask for the receipts themselves. The first reason for doing so is that this will tell you if the seller is actually keeping records of the expenses reported on the P&L. The second reason is that it will tell you if there are recurring expenses that should cause you concern, such as a plumber coming out every month to fix a toilet that was overflowing in unit six.

If you are using a CPA to do your tax returns, which you should always do, so as not to miss a deduction for which you are entitled, the accountant is going to need your receipts to complete your return. The seller should have this information because they would have had to give it to their CPA to prepare their return.

TIP 26

Make sure your seller isn't keeping two different sets of books.

There should not be one set of books for you and one for the IRS or the appraisal district. Seek open records requests from your governing body, which may have seller-provided financials that could be used to compare with the financials you are provided.

Harlan then corners June on the fact that there is nothing on her P&L that indicates that what she gave us was a pro forma or perspective spreadsheet and that it was presented as the actual financials from the property.

A. I told you this is—I did a retrospect.

Q. "Retrospective"—

A. Yeah.

Q. —is that the word you're looking for?

A. Yes, yes.

Q. And I don't mean to put words in your mouth, but—okay. But, again, nothing that shows that this is retrospective. Correct?

A. Yes.

Q. Does the income statement generated for the tax protest purposes more accurately match your tax return? Did I hear you say that a little earlier?

A. I don't remember.

Q. Okay. Well, we can look at them. (Feng Exhibit No. 6 marked.)

Q. (By Mr. Peabody) Mrs. Feng, do you recognize these as Shanghai Investments' tax returns?

A. Yes.

Q. And let's start out with the one on top, which is 2005. Do you recognize these as your tax returns?

A. Yeah.

Q. And if you go to—do you see at the bottom right-hand corner of the page, there are—there's a little label that says "SHANGHAI000519." Do you see that number?

A. Yeah.

Q. If you turn to SHANGHAI000523 for me, I'd like to ask you some questions about that.

A. (Complying.)

Q. Is that page that I'll call by shorthand page 523, is that the income report for Shanghai Investments for the year 2005?

A. Yeah.

Q. And that matches pretty closely what we looked at a minute ago as Exhibit No. 5. Correct? It shows total rent income on the tax return as $146,540. Is that right?

A. (Indicating.)

Q. On the tax return?

A. Yeah.

Q. And that's within $4,000 or $5,000 of the financial statement that you created for your tax protest. Correct?

A. Yeah.

Q. Okay. And it also shows that the Crestview Apartments had a loss that year of $22,350, correct?

Use a double-check system. If you get a profit and loss statement, ask for bank statements to confirm the amount of income the sellers are claiming.

TIP 27

Get a copy of the seller's Schedule E from his or her tax return.

This is an excellent way of verifying the information on the financials you are given. If the seller does not want to provide you with the Schedule E, you have to ask yourself what it is that the seller is trying to hide.

Harlan confronted June with the Fengs' bank statements, which also seemed commensurate with their tax returns and the financials they had given to the Nueces County Appraisal District in order to protest their tax returns:

Q. (By Mr. Peabody) Mrs. Feng, looking at Exhibit No. 7, the bank statements, Exhibit No. 7 starts at SHANGHAI000428 with a bank statement for February of 2005, and then the next pages through SHANGHAI000438 are the remaining cover sheets for the bank statements of the year 2005. Do you see that?

A. Yeah.

Q. When I added up the deposits that were made for the year 2005, I came up with $146,537. Now, I understand that you spent some cash before it was deposited into the bank, but that amount is roughly consistent with the revenue generated by the Crestview Apartments as reported to the IRS and as reported to the Nueces County Appraisal District, isn't it?

A. Yeah.

Q. And do you dis—I mean, we can add that number up if you want, but does that sound roughly right for the deposits made in 2005, $146,537?

A. (No response.)

Q. And if you want to get a calculator and add the deposits up for that year 2005, we can certainly do that. But does $146,537 sound about right to you as we sit here today for the deposits that you made for Crestview Apartments—

A. Yes.

Q. —rent?

A. Yes.

Q. Okay. And, again, that amount of bank deposits is well under half of the amount of rent reported on Exhibit 4, the typewritten 2005 profit-and-loss statement, which reported rent income of $338,654. Correct?

A. Yes.

Beware of unofficial financial statements!

TIP 28

Look for ways sellers' stories can be verified!

During June's deposition, Harlan questioned her on the vacancy reports she filed with Corpus Christi Water, and June admitted she falsified the number of vacancies on these reports in order to get a larger credit on her water bill. She also led Harlan to believe that it was the buyers' responsibility to investigate the property on their own and to not trust the information that they were given.

Q. You reported then—you reported to the City of Corpus Christi a false number for occupied and unoccupied units.
A. Yes.
Q. Correct?
A. Yeah.
Q. Because that would advantage you financially. Correct? Or could be used to advantage you financially?
A. Yes.
Q. Now, you want us to believe, though, that this September 6 rent roll marked as Exhibit 1 is an actually correct reflection of the number of occupied units?
A. (Indicating.)
Q. Exhibit No. 1.
A. Uh-huh.
Q. Is Exhibit No. 1 accurate?
A. Yes.
Q. And the report in Exhibit No. 15 is inaccurate?
A. That whole thing, the 2005, should be right. Two thousand six—maybe from the middle of 2006 until we sell it, not right.

Q. Okay. But you told them information that was not right anyway. Correct?

A. Yeah.

Q. Because you thought that might be to your benefit?

A. Yeah.

Q. In the same way it might be to your benefit to represent to the seller that the units were occupied when they were not. Correct?

A. Excuse me?

Q. It might also be to your benefit to tell a seller that units were occupied when they were not. Correct?

A. No. They can check. They can go there, check. They can drive around. They can check all the windows, knock on the doors. If they try to—if you want to buy a property, you're going to investigate.

Q. (By Mr. Peabody) So do you think that it is—do you think that it is true, that because a buyer could check to see whether any particular thing that you tell them is true or not, do you think that that absolves you from telling them the truth about it?

A. Can you ask me again?

Q. Okay. You said that a seller—a buyer could check to see whether units were occupied or unoccupied. Is that right?

A. Yes.

Q. And do you believe that because they could check, that that relieves you of any responsibility to tell them the truth about that thing that they could check about?

A. No.

When June created the falsified financials, she felt it was the buyer's responsibility to catch her lying. Everyone operates with a different set of values. We judged the Fengs by our set of values and integrity. We were not operating from the same playbook. Don't be naïve and believe that everyone thinks like you do!

TIP 29

Pay the price for a property on its performance not on what it looks like or what it could do.

As we closed out this line of questioning, Harlan continued to challenge June about her financial statements.

Q. Okay. And we have two reports that vary by a fairly significant degree, correct, for January of 2006?

A. With the water thing.

Q. The water thing and this rent roll?

A. Yes.

Q. Both of which were created by you to gain a financial advantage. In one case, to lower your water bill; in one case, to lower your tax bill. Is that correct?

A. Yes.

Q. Thinking about Exhibit No. 11, that's the 2006 profit-and-loss statement that you gave to Colonial Properties for use in connection with the sale of your property.

Mr. Hanson: What exhibit number?

Mr. Peabody: 11.

Q. (By Mr. Peabody) In January, you reported there rental income of $27,685. Correct?

A. Yes.

Q. Which, again, you said was based on a fully performing apartment building. Correct?

A. Yes.

Q. But it was actually only half full at the time?
A. Yes.

Its alright to pay a price greater than the property pencils out to be on paper but only do so if you know what the actual value really is!

TIP 30

Make sure that the monthly income from the rent roll equals the monthly reported income on the P&L statement. If they do not, this is a serious red flag!

Here is another connect-the-dots testimony. June's testimony and interaction with Isaac began as follows: June admitted that up until June 2006 the Crestview was and had been only about 50 percent occupied since their purchase in 2004. According to June, this property did not get allegedly "stabilized" until September or October, and yet Isaac was given the leases sometime after he and Garrett took the listing, which would have been around June or July 2006. If they had been given the leases then, it would have been apparent that they did not have sixty-six leases, so the building could not be 95 percent full as the Fengs had advertised in June 2006. As such they, Garrett and Isaac, would have known the financials they were freely distributing to potential buyers were fabricated.

Q. So if we wanted to go back now and compare this list to the leases of 2006, would you have those leases now?

A. When the time we give the copy to Isaac, we have a copy of that. I don't remember what date is that.

Q. A copy of?

A. Leases.

Q. Okay.

A. Yeah.

Q. Okay.

A. Before that, maybe already throw it away.

Q. Okay. So you think that the only copy of leases—well, you're saying you gave a copy of leases to Mr. Davis or Mr. Brewer at some point, but you don't have any others at this time. Is that correct?

After several attempts to rephrase this question let it suffice to say that Mrs. Feng no longer had copies of her leases and in fact had apparently thrown them away.

If the building was only half full in July 2006, then Garrett and Isaac would have only been given thirty-three leases. They would have known the building was only half full in spite of the P&L they were given.

TIP 31

Ask the agents for references.

Find out not only about the people who they sold for, but find out who bought from them. Ask them if they felt they were treated honestly and fairly. If you get the names of people they represented, you can always find out who the agents and their clients were on the other side. Beware of agents who straddle the line of right and wrong.

We felt we had enough to include Brewer and Davis in the lawsuit. They knew the Fengs, they knew the history of the property, they knew the Fengs' shoddy bookkeeping, and they were eyewitnesses to the condition of the property prior to Michael and me visiting: a building with boarded-up windows, trash, and abandoned vehicles.

We filed suit on Garrett and Isaac and deposed them on the first day of July 2009, at 9:35 a.m. It was two years since we took possession of the Crestview Apartments and a year after we filed our suit. We now had our first opportunity to question Davis and Brewer via their depositions. We were optimistic that we would get something we could sink our teeth into, some contradiction to information we'd been provided previously, and we did. Garrett was arrogant and glib throughout the entire interview, making sarcastic remarks and giving snide answers to every question.

Here's some of the typical exchange between Garrett and our attorney, Harlan Peabody:

Q. For people who don't know, would you describe the difference between a salesman's license and a brokerage license?

A. A salesman's license gives you the ability to sell real estate under a broker. And you are limited as to where you can go with a salesman's license, in that you always must be under the tutelage of a broker. With a brokerage license, you just have more leeway and more flexibility as to where you would like to go.

Q. When you say, "Where you would like to go," do you mean physically?

A. Yes. Physically, theoretically, yes, emotionally, mentally. I can go wherever you want. Float around.

Q. How many pieces of property have you sold since you've been at Colonial Properties?

A. I don't know. Quite a few.

Q. More than a hundred?

A. I don't know.

Q. (By Mr. Peabody) How many transactions do you handle in a typical year?

A. You know, in a high year, it's probably as many as fifteen transactions. And if we were to use a low year, being 2009, I would say two.

Q. Two for the entire year, or are you saying that you have handled two in this year, 2009, so far?

A. I have handled two so far this year.

Q. Not a good time to be in that business, is it?

A. If you want to make money, no. If you're in it just for sport, just to go get sued, then yes, it's probably a good time.

Q. Do you own any multifamily real estate yourself?

A. No.

Q. Have you ever?

A. Yes.

Q. When did you first buy an apartment building or a multifamily project?

A. Probably 19—approximately 1991.

Q. Will you describe that piece of property to me?

A. That piece of property was a fourplex.

Q. How long did you own it?

A. A few years.

Q. Two, three?

A. Five. And I'll preface, I don't know that it's been five years. I'm just pulling a number out of my ass. It might be four; it might have been seven, if you're asking for a time.

As Harlan gathered information, we found out that not only did Garrett have firsthand knowledge of the management of apartment

buildings, but he had twenty years of experience in doing so. He had been
a licensed agent for fifteen years, and for five years prior to that, he was
a property manager and owner of over seventy apartment units himself!
How could he not tell a property was only 50 percent occupied?

**Harlan then asked Garrett what information would be the first thing
he'd ask for as an agent selling an income-producing property.**

Q. Once you have a listing agreement, and you have a formal contract
between yourself and your client, what kind of information do you ask them
to provide you about the property?

A. Profit and loss statements, rent rolls, current rent roll. And then ultimately will ask them for pertinent information, you know, about the property
itself.

Q. You ask for profit and loss statements. Do you ask for a current one
only or do you want to go back in time?

A. No. You know, a year and a half to two years.

Q. Are most of your sellers able to provide you that information pretty
timely?

A. Yes.

Q. Does it take a lot of time or weeks to get it to you?

A. Sometimes it's like that, (finger clicking), ten within minutes.
Sometimes it takes days, weeks. Just depends. Certainly days.

Q. You said you ask for current rent rolls. Do you ask for historical information on rent rolls as well?

A. Generally not.

Q. Those are things you know that buyers are going to want to know
about. They're going to want to know about the ability of the property to
produce income?

A. Buyers and potential lenders, yes.

Q. And same with rent rolls. They're going to want to know the occupancy rates?

A. Yes.

Q. The buyers are interested in that?

A. Yes.

Q. And it's important that that stuff is accurate?

A. Yes.

Harlan continued with questions about how the price was set. Garrett detailed how a listing price was determined by analyzing rent rolls and profit and loss statements, and by walking the grounds.

We now know that the Fengs never turned over a profit and loss statement or a rent roll to either he or Isaac until August, nearly ten weeks after they had already established the price of the complex on the listing agreement, which makes you wonder what they used to establish the price in late June. Would the delay in producing the financials not have caused a "seasoned" agent to question why the Feng's would need this long to fabricate a profit and loss statement?

TIP 32

Check the dates on when documents are created.

If you receive a rent roll for December, it should have been created at the end of December or January, not in May. Dates that don't coincide could imply that these documents were fabricated.

The line of questioning now centered on the listing agreement Brewer and Davis had with the Fengs.

Q. This is dated July 1 on the part of the Fengs and July 6 on the part of Mr. Davis. Do you remember that as being about the right time for this sale?

A. I would say, based on looking at this, I would say that that would be the exact time.

Q. This lists the purchase price for the property as $1,730,000, correct?

A. That is correct.

Q. How does a purchase price like that get established—or how did this purchase price get established? Let me ask a more specific question.

A. This purchase price would have been established by looking at the operating numbers, the profit and loss that would have been provided by the seller to us. And we would have done some underwriting on it and come up with a determination as to what we thought the property would bear out on the market. And it was obviously then an agreeable number with the Fengs.

Q. And you remember that process taking place in this instance?

A. I don't remember the specific detail of it, but I know the process.

Q. And that process took place in this case?

A. Obviously so, yes.

Q. Do you know what profit and loss statements you had in July of 2006—

A. No.

Q. —for this piece of property?

A. No.

Q. Does Colonial Properties preserve those kind of records?

A. Isaac and I preserve those kind of records that we would have had.

Q. Did you review anything today before you came to your deposition?

A. No.

Q. Didn't look at any documents?

A. We looked at our marketing flyer. We did look at that.

Q. Do you remember when you first got a profit and loss statement from the Fengs?

A. No.

Q. Is it fair to say that you must have had them at the time that this listing agreement was entered into?

A. I would say that would be a fair assessment.

Q. If you had those in your files, they would still be there, is that right?

A. Yes. They would. If I had them in my files, they would be probably in your files and Pamela's files and the Fengs' attorneys' files.

Q. You anticipated my next question.

A. There we go.

Q. You have given those materials to your attorney, is that correct?

A. I have indeed.

Q. Have you given her everything that you have—

A. I have indeed.

Q. —regarding—

A. Oh, excuse me.

Q. That's okay. You've given her everything you have regarding this transaction, the Crestview sale?

A. Yes.

Q. Did you keep any of those materials on a computer on a hard drive?

A. Yes.

Q. Have you made those materials available to her as well?

A. Yes.

Q. Describe the analysis that you go through in setting a purchase price. You said you look at the profit and loss statements. You do some underwriting. What does that mean?

A. It means looking at some historical operating information, whatever the period of time is that we have been provided and are working off of. And then we look at the historical, we take the rent rolls, so that we can see a snapshot of what the property may be doing most immediately so that we are not underwriting the property on historical income numbers. We're underwriting on current income. Or at least analyzing how it's performing currently versus how it has performed historically on the income side. And then we look at the expenses. And again, depending on the period of time that we're looking at, we want to have ideally a full year's worth of expenses so that we have a full picture of what the expenses actually are over the year. And see how that performs. And then we also run a pro forma of the income and expense to see, you know, how the property might perform under, you know, a possible scenario of operation. And in many cases we find a property on the expense side may be running inordinately low or inordinately high on the expenses. And we'll make adjustments to the expense side of the equation. We adjust for taxes and insurance to bring them up to, or down, as the case may be, but generally up to what the current market levels are and the levels at which lenders are underwriting.

This may be a little bit more challenging to do but if you ask to see the financials that were used to establish the sales price of the property and you are able to get them you can always check the meta data to see when they were created. If the financials were dated after the selling price was set you should ask questions. We now knew the first financials that Isaac and Garrett were given were not created until August 11, 2006. This was a full five weeks after the listing agreement and the price was established on July 6.

We believe, in our case, the value of the building was set, and then the financials were constructed to justify the price after the fact.

TIP 33

Ask the agent what information was used in determining the asking price.

If agents used historical performance, they should be able to back up their figures. They should also be able to provide the source documents for this documents they provide you.

Harlan carries on with his interrogation of Garrett Brewer:

Q. So if the profit and loss statement was inaccurate, the occupancy that you extrapolate by that means would also be inaccurate, is that correct?

A. Assuming that it's inaccurate, yes.

Q. Do you know if that's how you did it in this case?

A. Made assumptions on inaccurate information?

Q. No. Made assumptions on the occupancy rate by looking at the profit and loss statement.

A. I don't recall.

Q. Did you know anything about the historical performance of the Crestview Apartments when you were initially involved in this listing?

A. I'm sure I knew something. I don't recall what the actual occupancy issues were.

Q. Do you remember the occupancy rate of the property when you took the listing?

A. I do not.

Q. Do you rely solely on what the sellers of property tell you about occupancy rates?

A. Specific to their property, yes.

Q. Do you visit the property when you take a listing?

A. I visit the property.

Q. What do you do when you make that sort of visit?

A. Go out, see the property, walk a couple units, usually a vacant unit, maybe some occupied units. But, you know, just a little sampling of them, couple, three, four units to get a feel for what the interiors look like.

Q. Did you do that in this case?

A. I would have done that, yes.

Q. Do you remember doing that?

A. Specifically, no.

Q. What were your impressions of the Crestview Apartments in June and July of 2006?

A. That it was a pretty dumpy complex, that the owners were poor boying. They were not really putting much money back into the property.

Q. When you say "poor boying," what do you mean by that term?

A. As I just said. They were not putting much money back into the property.

Q. Was it in poor condition?

A. Yes. It was in poor condition.

Q. What things specifically did you notice that makes you believe—that makes you say it was in poor condition?

A. The swimming pool that was shut down and falling apart. And the roofs on the property were in mediocre condition at best. The air conditioning units were in mediocre condition. The interior of the units occupied and units that were vacant were in mediocre to poor condition. There were cockroaches present in the property.

Q. Would you say that relative to other similar properties, it was in worse condition than those—

A. To similar property, no. I would say they would be similar.

Q. May have been a bad question, because I asked you, "Was it similar to similar properties?" Relative to other properties of its kind, was it in better or worse condition or about the same?

A. I've seen much worse. I've seen much better. You know, for that type of property, it was fairly similar.

The agents should not only be able to support how the asking price was calculated; they should be able to show you supporting evidence that similar properties in the same area of town that were performing in the same fashion sold for the same price.

If an agent tells you that they visited 5 vacant units in a 20 unit complex and they told you there was only a 5% vacancy rate you should suspect foul. Five vacant units out of 20 would represent a 25% vacancy factor.

In our case had Isaac walked anymore than 4 units he would have known that the vacancy rate was greater than the 5% vacancy the Feng's reported.

TIP 34

Find out the occupancy levels of similar types of properties in the city in which you are considering a purchase.

If your subject property is dramatically higher or lower than the market, find out why. Are the rents higher or lower than the rest of their competition? If there is no logical explanation as to why the subject property is outperforming similar properties in the same city, you might question the legitimacy of the seller's information. A good source for this information would be market survey companies and the local appraisal district.

At this point, however, our legal strategy went astray. As mentioned in the introduction, a party can be guilty of statutory fraud by knowingly passing along false information, but instead Mr. Peabody spent the next four hours trying to get Garrett to admit he had a hand in creating the rent rolls and profit and loss statements, which Garrett would not oblige him. The financial statements we were given were not produced until August 10th five weeks after the Fengs signed the listing agreement with Colonial. Garret stated that they would have relied upon the Feng's financials to determine the asking price for the Crestview Apartments. However, in this case, the sales price was already determined on the July 6th listing agreement was established well over a month before the Feng's financials were turned over to their agents.

Unless the property in which you have interest offers some tremendous benefit of amenities, extremely low rent, or some other feature, there is no reason that its occupancy level should be 15 to 20 percent higher than similar properties.

TIP 35

Question everything!

It is one thing for a seller to accidently or deliberately omit items that should be on a P&L but it is another thing if the agent allows these financials to be sent to prospective buyers without ensuring that all the items that should be on a profit and loss statement are in fact there. If the agent allows documents a perspective buyer would rely upon in making a decision to purchase be passed along as fact the agent is guilty of gross negligence if not fraud. The agent has a legal responsibility to not perpetrate what they know or should know as fraud to the public. Such an act is careless, ignorant, or intentional in which the agent is trying to wash his hands of the deal and to not appear as they've had any hand in helping his clients provide inaccurate financial documents. In our case, the sellers' agents were not just agents but brokers, brokers who in fact had owned multifamily properties themselves. Could we have done a better job? Yes, we could have. Did we trust too much? Yes, we did. Would we do differently in the future now, having the benefit of doing a forensic analysis of this transaction? Absolutely we would!

Don't let your emotions get the best of you! Don't overlook the obvious!

The deposition of Isaac Davis

So on July 2, 2009, at 9:22 a.m., we deposed Isaac. After Harlan wasted the better part of an hour trying to get Isaac to admit he made up the numbers on the financials to no avail, he brought up the topic of the decommissioned pool that Garrett also mentioned during his deposition.

Isaac said, "So there was the pool thing, which Garrett Brewer brought up yesterday. You know, the pool had been drained. And they put some boards in there, something to cover it up. And that's not uncommon at all with 'C' class property or even 'B' class properties. For some folks, it's just a liability to have a pool. And so they fill them in—drain them, and fill them in."

We also learned from Isaac during his deposition that the Fengs installed submeters on the property during their ownership, which cost several thousand dollars. The Fengs never reported this on their profit and loss statement, which would have affected the valuation of the property. Isaac, who apparently knew this information passed it on in the form of the the P&L to us without disclosing this fact.

Isaac said, "The only thing that really sticks out in my mind that was a major deal, I think they installed the submeters. And I'm not 100 percent sure they did that. It might have been the previous owner. But I think they might have actually installed the submeters for the electric, which would have been a big expense. And again, I'm not 100 percent sure they did that. But I think, I think that was done when they owned it."

If this type of capital improvement was done on the property, why did Isaac not question why it did not appear on the Fengs' P&L statement?

TIP 36

Beware of operating expenses
that are too low!

This is true even if the owner is living onsite and personally doing most of the work. There are certain things that the average owner is not qualified to do, including electrical, plumbing, drain service, utilities, pest control, purchase appliances and appliance service, HVAC, and locksmith work. No matter how efficiently a property is being run, over the long haul it will require some or all of these services. This is exactly the reason to get two years of financials. It seemed apparent that both Garrett and Isaac felt that as long as they had something in writing from their sellers, no matter how false it was from their own observations, they felt they had no duty to protect the public by sharing this information.

Isaac continued by describing the cleanliness of the units he visited on the property, which was vastly different than the account given by the rest of our witnesses.

Q. Do you remember the general cleanliness of the apartments when you took the listing?

A. Yes. I do. And I was surprised. They were a lot cleaner than I was expecting them to be. Again, I only probably walked five, six units. I just saw a sampling of some of the vacants. And the ones that I saw were very—they were vacant; they were made ready. They were clean.

Make sure you review all aspects of the data you've been given. If you were told in the marketing material for the property that its occupancy level was 95% then get rent rolls for the last year to verify this. Get the profit and loss statements for the last year to confirm the income they've reported is true.

Calculate how many occupied or vacant units would substantiate this statement. During his deposition Isaac stated he visited 5 or 6 vacant unit, which was a sampling of the vacant units. Even with 5 vacant units the occupancy would have only been 91% and at 6 units it would only be 90%. This may not seem to be a big deal but with an average rent of $500/mo. this affected the cash flow by $2000 per month or $24,000 per year. Assuming the vacancies were only limited to six units and not more as we later discovered and with the prevailing CAP rate this would have reduced the value of the property by $250,000.

As an investor you need to verify and cross check everything!

TIP 37

Inspect every unit with an inspector and make sure you are not only identifying deferred maintenance but also verifying that there is a tenant in every unit in which the rent roll states there is.

In the discovery phase of litigation, we uncovered some information that led to an entirely separate line of questioning in and of its own. One of the most incriminating pieces of evidence we found was an offer from another agent for the Crestview written in October 2006, over a month before I came to Corpus Christi. As it was a full-priced offer, we were curious as to why the sale was not consummated, and, more importantly, what the property looked like six weeks before we were on the grounds. The offer was written by a new agent, Junior Garces, that was working under the direction of an experienced multifamily agent, Jenna Valdez. Junior had written his cell phone number on the contract, and fortunately for us the number still worked. When I made contact with him, he told me that Jenna was really the agent on the deal and that I needed to speak with her.

I must have called Jenna a dozen times. She was curt and impatient, and even though I explained how important her testimony of this transaction was to our lawsuit, she definitely did not want to get involved and ignored the rest of my calls. As we came to find out, there was a definite reluctance of one agent to "out" a fellow agent, as we tried to solicit other expert witnesses in the field. It was not until I wrote Jenna a letter appealing to the value she placed upon family and how this crime had decimated our families that she agreed to give her testimony in a deposition.

So on July 26, 2010, at 10:08 a.m., Jenna came into the office of Harlan Peabody, our attorney, to provide her testimony. The condition of the

Crestview that she witnessed was diametrically opposed to the one we saw only a month later. What she saw was boarded-up units, abandoned vehicles, and generally a building in a sorry state of disrepair. It initially took Jenna time to find the location of the Crestview, as the listing on Loopnet, which was an Internet site Colonial Properties used to market the property, advertised the property with a fictitious address.

The phony address was in the middle of a vacant field on the outskirts of town belonging to a local cargo handling company. Jenna, being a local agent, knew where the building was and found it in spite of the fictitious address given in the listing.

The following is an account of Jenna's first impression of the listing for the Crestview Apartments that Colonial Properties put on the Internet and her subsequent visit to the complex. Tips 38-46 are Jenna's subsequent discoveries.

TIP 38

Find out among recent sales what income other similar properties reported.

Harlan Peabody begins his series of questions…

Q. Okay. Do you know why the Crestview Apartments was attractive to Mr. Sanchez (her client) as a prospect?

A. Okay. I remember looking at the numbers, and we sat down, and we looked at the numbers, and the numbers were incredible.

Q. Okay.

A. More than other apartments themselves.

Q. Okay …

Q. (By Mr. Peabody) And what numbers were you looking at when you made those determinations?

A. There were some numbers on LoopNet.

Q. Okay. Specifically, can you remember—and you may refer back to Exhibit No. 1, if you like—what numbers seemed particularly attractive to you?

A. Well, the gross income, the expenses.

Q. And—and—again, I'm going to interrupt you for a moment. I know I said I would try not to do that, but, again, because we're taking down and making video, what you're—are you looking at what page of this LoopNet listing?

A. Page 2.

Q. Okay. And I'm sorry for interrupting you. I just wanted to make that clear.

A. No problem.

Q. What numbers or what information was particularly interesting and attractive to you in terms of this property?

A. The second page where it shows the income, expenses, operating income. When you do the numbers, and you see the unit numbers, and you see how many units were, I mean, it just looked—it looked very promising.

Q. (By Mr. Peabody) Okay. And what was very promising about those numbers?

A. There was positive income.

Q. Okay. Was it better than similarly sized apartment units?

A. Most definitely.

Q. Okay. How much better? And I'm not asking for sort of percentages, but what was—what was your—your impression?

A. Well, it was so much better that we had thirty, forty apartments to go show him. And that was the first one that he wanted to go see because he didn't want it to slip away if it was that good.

Q. (By Mr. Peabody) Okay. Were there any other pieces of information on the LoopNet listing that you thought were particularly interesting or made the Crestview Apartments particularly attractive from a buyer's point of view?

A. We didn't get that until after we saw the property itself.

Q. Okay. What about the occupancy rates? Was there anything about the occupancy rates on the LoopNet listing that—

A. Most definitely. Now, that, I remember for sure. It said—

Q. Okay. And what do you remember about that?

A. It said that the occupancy rate was very, very high. And when we got there, it was not that high.

Q. Okay. If you would look at that listing, the LoopNet listing, do you see the occupancy rate there?

A. It's very blurry. No.

Q. If you wouldn't mind looking about the middle block of the middle of the page.

A. Yes, yes, yes, yes.

Q. What occupancy rate is listed on the LoopNet?

A. Ninety-five percent.

Q. Okay. How does that compare to other apartment complexes of similar type?

A. Well, there was a lot—

Q. (By Mr. Peabody) Yes, ma'am.

A. Okay. There was a lot of other ones that would say 80, 75, 82, 85. I mean, and that's pretty much normal when you're looking at a commercial real estate apartment unit. When we saw 95 percent, and then we looked at page 2, and we saw, you know, how much income was coming in, we said, this is—this is a deal, you know, and that's why we went to go look at it right away.

Properties in similar neighborhoods should be selling for similar prices. It is difficult to believe that any one property in the same category of apartments would be significantly better than others. They could be significantly lower, yes, but significantly better, no.

The income and expenses determine the net operating income (NOI), and when you divide this by the capitalization rate (cap rate), or the rate of expected return for similar properties in a similar market, you can calculate the value. Once you have the value, you can divide the number of units into this figure and come up with a value per door. You should be wary of a property in a neighborhood that is selling for $25,000 per door when the rest of the properties in the neighborhood were selling for $12,000, as ours had only two years earlier.

TIP 39

Look for pride of ownership or signs that tenants are proud to live there.

One of the main reasons Jenna's client wanted to get the Crestview Apartments under contract was because of the high occupancy figures the marketing material from Colonial Properties boasted.

Once Jenna and her clients visited the property, they had a totally different impression.

Q. (By Mr. Peabody) What did you notice about the apartment—tell me what—what did you see when you got to the Crestview Apartments with Mr. Sanchez?

A. When we looked from the street, it looked—it looked okay. So we drove to the back, so we could park our car. And do you want me to be detailed or—

A. I remember going in and on my right-hand side there was, like, a—like, a structure, you know, where—no, it wasn't a structure. It was, like, concrete where a structure used to be.

Q. Uh-huh.

A. And you could tell that maybe it was torn down or burned down or—that caught our eye because we were, like, were there apartments there or what's going on? We saw a lot of cars standing up on blocks, you know, with no tires or anything like that. That caught our eye.

Q. What—what about—

A. We saw a lot of apartment complexes.

Q. (By Mr. Peabody) Let me—let me—let me interrupt and ask you about those cars. What about seeing cars on blocks—what significance would that have for you as a—as a seller of real estate?

A. It has a lot to do with it. I mean, it tells you—it tells you that the people that live there—I don't know. I don't want to say something wrong.

Q. No. You can—you should just say what's—you know and what's true. You won't say anything wrong.

A. It tells you a lot about the people that live there and how well taken care of their apartments were and the kind of management the apartments had.

Q. Okay. Would that be—

Q. (By Mr. Peabody) Would that be a positive factor?

A. Not at all.

Q. Okay. Would it be a negative factor?

A. Yes, most definitely.

Q. What does it tell you about the management, for example?

A. That it wasn't good at all. I mean—

A. There was—there wasn't just one car on blocks. There was—there was a lot. There was a lot of cars with broken windows. So we didn't know if a lot of vandalism was going on in that apartment complex. And that—you know—we didn't know what was going on. And then when we went to the back of the building, and we saw a lot of the windows boarded up and—

Q. (By Mr. Peabody) What windows did you see that were boarded up?

A. The back of the building, not the front of the—there's two—I remember there was two sections and in the middle of the—of the apartment complex is where the parking lot was. It was the building in the back.

Jenna went on to recount her observations of the boarded-up units.

Q. Okay. Now, you mentioned seeing some apartment units with boards. Can you indicate on that drawing of the Crestview Apartments which units had boards on them?

A. Do you want me to give you numbers?

Q. Sure. That would help because it will help anybody who's looking at this later understand what you're talking about.

A. 501, 503, 505, 507, 509, and 511. Now, I can't tell you that all of them had boards, but that's the section where the boards were.

Q. Okay.

Mr. Mesero: Pardon me. Hold on real quick. Could you repeat those numbers, please?

The witness: Most definitely: 501, 503, 505, 507, 509, 511.

Q. (By Mr. Peabody) Okay. Did any of the other buildings that you noticed that day have boarded-up units?

A. Some in the front, but not a lot. I remember in the back there was
plenty.

Q. And in the front, what building—what—what numbers of the units
are in that front building, again, just so that somebody who's reading this or
hearing this later can understand what you're indicating?

A. Can I ask you a question to be able to answer that?

Q. Yeah.

A. Where is the office?

Q. I'm not sure which one of those is the office, but if you could just sort
of indicate by—you know—these buildings all—you know—in one building,
all the units start with a number one and in other buildings they start with
fours, twos, sevens, and fives as you noticed before.

A. It was the farthest one from the office.

Q. (By Mr. Peabody) If you can use maybe a system like that to describe
where you saw other boarded-up units.

A. 129 and 127.

Q. Okay. Do you have any—do you remember today, approximately, how
many units had boards on them?

A. Ten, twelve. We went into a unit right next to one that had a board.

Q. Okay.

Q. (By Mr. Peabody) It's all right. About ten or twelve units had boards?

A. Correct.

*Are the grounds clean, porches decorated with plants, or signs that
someone considers this his or her home? It doesn't have to be an expensive
home for people to be proud of where they live. Does the property look like
people have been and intend to stay there for a while? Or, with a couple
of garbage bags, could they pack up everything they own and move in
thirty minutes? If a family came on the property with children, is it an
environment where they would feel safe?*

*People that live in a complex with crime, abandoned vehicles, and
garbage do not have pride in where they live but rather live in fear and
hide in their apartments, as they have nowhere else to go.*

TIP 40

Remember when you're purchasing a multi-family property your purchasing the performance of the property over a period of time and not just what it is doing on the day you look at it.

Q. (By Mr. Peabody) Other than the units that were boarded up, did you have any—did you make any observations that would allow you to estimate how many of the other units might have been occupied?

A. We talked to some people that lived there.

Q. (By Mr. Peabody) Okay. What did you talk to those people about?

A. We asked them how the management was in the apartment building. We asked them if their apartment building—not the apartment building. I'm sorry.—their apartment unit was well taken care of inside. And we had several responses because we spoke to—I can't tell you exactly how many, but it was three, four predominantly black people. And they told us that the apartment buildings in the back had been boarded up for quite a while.

A. And that wasn't the last time I went to the property.

Q. Okay.

A. I went to the property, but it wasn't for Mr. Sanchez.

Q. All right.

Q. (By Mr. Peabody) I was getting to that, actually.

A. Okay.

Q. You went a week later. Did you ever go again?

A. I did.

Q. For what purpose?

A. With another client.

Q. Okay. Do you know when that was?

A. I don't remember if it was in December or January. I—I—I couldn't tell you. We never did a contract or anything like that, but we did take a client to go look at the property.

Q. (By Mr. Peabody) Was that in December of 2006?

A. Yes, sir.

Q. What was the condition of the property then?

A. I don't think it was the same.

Q. (By Mr. Peabody) In what way was it different?

A. They didn't have the—they didn't have the cars on blocks.

Q. Any other changes?

A. There wasn't all the apartment buildings in the back boarded up.

Q. When you went back in December, did you go into any of those—

A. No, I did not.

Q. —units? And, again, I'll scold you a little bit. If you'll let me finish—

A. Sorry.

Q. —just, again, so that it's clear.

A. Sorry.

Q. No. It's quite all right. Let me just ask again, so that it's clear: When you went back in December of 2006 or January of 2007, did you go into any of those boarded units?

A. No, sir.

Q. Okay. Did you go into any units at that time?

A. No, sir.

Q. Okay.

A. We went to the office.

Q. Okay. What about the condition of the roofs … in December of 2006, do you—do you remember if there was any difference there?

A. I don't recall.

Q. Okay. Had the property been repainted?

A. Yes.

Q. Now, turning back to the time that you were there with Mr. Sanchez in roughly October, did you get any other financial information about the Crestview Apartments from Mr. Feng when you were there?

A. From Mr. Feng?

Q. Uh-huh.

A. Yes, we did.

Q. What did you get from him?

A. Well, he told us that—we asked for, you know, rent, utility, a lot of numbers. And he told us that they were updating everything on LoopNet. And I asked him, I said, "So the numbers are not correct on LoopNet right now?" And he said that they were updating everything and making some changes on LoopNet, so for me to call the brokers next week, and they'd be able to give me all that information.

Q. Okay.

Q. (By Mr. Peabody) Did Mr. Feng give you any additional updated financial information when you were there?

A. We asked him why it said that it was so highly occupied, and it wasn't. He said that there was going to be some changes on LoopNet. That's when he told us that they were updating everything on LoopNet as it was.

Q. (By Mr. Peabody) Let me ask you this: Based on your observation of the property in October of 2006, do you think that the occupancy rate described on LoopNet was accurate?

A. Not at all.

Q. (By Mr. Peabody) What made you have that view?

A. Well—

A. —because—I mean, just by going—we walked the whole apartment complex when we were there. You could tell it was not 95 percent. It doesn't take a genius to figure that out.

Q. (By Mr. Peabody) And about how many apartment buildings had you shown or looked at at the time that you showed Mr. Sanchez the Crestview Apartments?

A. Plenty.

Q. More—

A. How many?

Q. More than fifty?

A. Oh, yes.

Q. More than a hundred?

A. No.

Q. Say, between fifty and a hundred?

A. Yes, sir.

Q. Did you ask Mr. Feng about the discrepancy between the 95 percent occupancy rate and what you observed?

A. Yes, sir.

Q. (By Mr. Peabody) What did Mr. Feng tell you?

A. That was being updated by LoopNet because he didn't know if that number was correct.

Q. (By Mr. Peabody) Okay. Did he tell you that number was not correct?

A. He told me that he didn't—we asked him, "Why are all those apartment buildings in the back boarded up. There's no way that it could be 95 percent." And we showed him this because we took it with us for the directions and—

Q. And "this" is Exhibit No. 1?

A. Yes, sir.

Q. (By Mr. Peabody) Okay. Go on, please.

A. I forgot what I was saying.

Q. That's all right. Did you—did you ask Mr. Feng about the difference between the 95 percent reported occupancy on LoopNet and what you saw?

A. Yes, I did.

Q. (By Mr. Peabody) And what did he say about that?

A. He said that he did not think that was correct, and they were updating it on LoopNet.

Q. Okay. When you say "that was correct," what—

A. Ninety-five percent.

Q. Okay. Did you ask Mr. Feng how the LoopNet listing came to have 95 percent occupancy listed on it?

A. Well, no. I asked him if the brokers that were working on the—on the LoopNet were the ones that were listed there, or had it changed. Because when he told me they were updating it, I didn't understand how they could be updating it if all the numbers were already there.

A. So I asked him if he had changed brokers and maybe that's why it was getting updated by a different company. And he said that, no, that that was Colonial Properties that was doing the updating on the computer, which I didn't—I didn't understand.

Q. (By Mr. Peabody) Okay. Did Mr. Feng have any—any documents, any pieces of paper, to give you about the financial performance of the Crestview Apartments when you were there with Mr. Sanchez?

A. No, sir.

Q. Did you ask for any?

A. He said that they had them, (and) that I needed to get in touch with Colonial because they were updating everything.

Q. (By Mr. Peabody) Did you try to get with anybody at Colonial Properties to get those items?

A. I did.

Remember the performance of a multifamily asset is a movie not a picture. It is the performance of the property over several months. What we had in our case is that when the Feng's listed the Crestview with Colonial in July of 2006 by June Feng's testimony the property was roughly 50% occupied. The property was placed on Loopnet by Colonial in October of 2006 boasting 95% occupancy. The property was visited by Jenna Valdez in October shortly after the listing was placed on the internet. What she witnessed was abandoned vehicles, 10 or more units boarded up and the owners had no financials to share.

When Jenna visited in December she viewed a freshly painted property, no boards, no abandoned vehicles which gave the income statement credibility.

The condition of the property, the low vacancy, the boarded up units, the trash and the abandoned vehicles and then the subsequent improvements that were done to improve the appearance of the property were all part of the movie.

The freshly manicured grounds and newly painted buildings Jenna witnessed in December and what I observed during my visit in November were only a picture.

Remember you are buying long term performance and the longer the asset has been performing the more valuable it is! Talk to people (i.e. the postman, the local police department, fire and code officers) that can show you the movie not just a picture!!

TIP 41

The tenants are your best witnesses.

Q. Okay. Did he open up any of the boarded-up five units?

A. No. He would not. He said that—

Q. Okay.

A. —they were not in livable condition, that they were going to fix them.

Q. Okay.

Q. (By Mr. Peabody) Okay. Do you know how many of the units were being remodeled?

A. He said that the most part of the back were being remodeled at the time. And that's when we asked why there were so many that were boarded up. And he said that every single time he would remodel, he would board them up so that nobody would go in when they were fixing them up.

Units do not become vacant overnight neither do major remodels. The best and one of the most impartial set of witnesses are the existing tenants. They've presumably lived on the property for weeks if not years. Interview them and when you do find out if all their appliances are in good working order. Ask them if maintenance requests are addressed promptly. Find out if the property is quiet, and curfew is maintained. Ask the tenants if they feel safe at the complex. Compare the rent rolls for changes in tenant names. If tenants are coming and going, and the owners are taking good care of the property, they will be spending money on flooring, appliances, and paint. If they are not, they are moving new people into the units in uninhabitable conditions. No one knows the history of a complex better than the tenants.

Also, review the financials to see how much is being spent on appliances, carpet, paint, etc. Poorly maintained units breed unhappy tenants, and unhappy tenants breed high turnover and vacancies. When you go in to contract order an inspection to go through all the units to assess the deferred maintenance so you get a feeling for what you're getting yourself into and most importantly attend the inspections! Had we attended ours, and knowing what I know now I am convinced the sellers and the agents would have panicked and canceled the deal for fear of being unmasked.

If the owner does not take pride in the property, you can never expect the tenants to do so.

TIP 42

When you walk the property you are considering, compare the number of vacant units with the rent roll.

The deposition of Jenna Valdez continued.

Q. (By Mr. Peabody) How many units did you go into?
A. Two.
Q. Okay. What was the condition of those units?
A. I almost threw up.
Q. Really? Why is that?
A. Because they smelled like urine.
Q. (By Mr. Peabody) I'm sorry. I couldn't hear you.
A. They smelled like urine.
Q. Were they dirty?
A. Very.
Q. Other than smelling like urine, was there other trash in them?
A. The carpet was—
A. The carpet was very—in very bad shape. I remember one of the units had the dishwasher taken out, and there was water all around it. We asked what had happened. And they said that they were in the process of remodeling a lot of the units.

Insist on examining every unit. Examination of every unit can not only validate the occupancy but also identify the deferred maintenance needing to be completed on the complex. The observable evidence of a neglected property should alert the buyer of potential maintenance that may not be readily visible.

Even if you cannot get the specific unit numbers, ask the agent or owner how many units are vacant and see if that is commensurate with the total numbers on the rent roll that you were given.

TIP 43

No one should have to "work" on the numbers.

Harlan continues to question Jenna on the information she was hoping to have received.

Q. What would you like-d to have seen?

A. I wanted to see numbers. I wanted to get utilities. I wanted to get specifics on the property. And every single time they would tell me that they would give them to me, they would give them to me, and I never received anything. They told me that all they had for right now was what was on LoopNet because they were working with Mr. Feng.

Q. (By Mr. Peabody) Okay. Now, you said you wanted to get numbers, and I think you mentioned utilities, in particular. What—what—what does that mean? When you say you wanted to get utilities, what specifically did you want to be given?

A. When you show a commercial listing, you want to see utilities for how many units the place has, and that way you can get a very close figure to what the occupancy is.

Q. Okay.

A. In other words, if you get utilities for—if there's a hundred units in the apartment building and you get utilities for ninety-six, then you know it's pretty—you know—pretty close. But if you get utilities for forty, then you know there's a problem.

Q. Okay.

Q. (By Mr. Peabody) Did you ever get any—any information about the utility usage at the Crestview Apartments?

A. No, we did not.

If the property is not master-metered, call the utility company and see if you can find out how many bills they've issued to the property each month for the last year. This will give you a pretty good idea of the true occupancy of the property. If the property is master-metered and the seller tells you the occupancy has been increasing however the utility bill has not gone up as well this should be suspect.

If the property was master-metered as was the Crestview, and if the owner was billing the tenants back for their portion of the utilities, the owner should be able to produce two years of invoices he or she had prepared for the tenants for their portion of the utilities. If the tenants are billed directly by the utility company, you can call the utility company, and you may not be able to get the names or amounts, but you should be able to find out how many tenants were billed each month. If the number of bills does not equal the number of names on the rent rolls, you should be highly suspicious.

Lastly, If sellers are serious about selling their property, they should have financials to share, especially five months into the listing. The sellers should not be relying upon their agents to trump up the financials, particularly if the agents were not their property managers and not responsible for either collecting rents or paying the bills on the property.

In states where the property taxes are adjusted annually one should check with the county assessor's office to see if they've conducted market survey's on occupancy levels. In many municipalities assessors make a practice of surveying properties as that is part of how the tax basis for the buildings is calculated.

We did not discover that Nuces County had this practice until after we were involved in this lawsuit and discovered that the average occupancy rate for this part of Corpus Christi was 84 percent. Had we known this we certainly would have insisted the Feng's provide more proof why their building was at 95%, a full 11 points higher than similar properties. We would not have accepted the Fengs' financials indicating their property had been at 95 percent without at least asking why.

TIP 44

The names on the invoices should match up with the names on the rent rolls.

Q. (By Mr. Peabody) What other pieces of information, other than information about utility usage, would have you liked to have gotten about the Crestview Apartments?

A. We wanted figures to prove that that was correct. We wanted to see papers. We wanted to see their expenses. They—this—we want—

Q. Now, you're pointing at the LoopNet listing. And I don't mean to fuss at you—

A. Yes, sir.

Q. —but, again, just so that we're clear later, what numbers are you pointing at, at the—

A. Effective gross income, total expense. We wanted them to show us. Because they kept telling us that they were doing a lot of remodeling and that was a lot of their expenses, so we wanted to see it on paper. We wanted them to show us exactly what they were talking about.

Q. (By Mr. Peabody) Okay. Did you ask for financial statements?

A. We did. We asked for financial statements quite awhile—quite a bit. And everything was going to be given to us at a later moment.

A. After we put in the contract, we told them that we had ten days to get those financial—

Q. (By Mr. Peabody) Okay.

Q. (By Mr. Peabody) Who did you ask for financial statements?

A. The broker. I do not remember his name.

Q. Okay. And, again, if you don't remember the name of the person you talked to, what I mean is, is, you know, did you ask Mr. Feng, did you ask somebody at Colonial Properties, did you ask some guy you met at the coffee shop? I'm just—you know—just generally speaking—

A. Yes, sir.

Q. —you know—even if you don't know the name of the person you talked to, I'm trying to figure out where you made that inquiry.

A. Yes, sir.

Q. (By Mr. Peabody) Did you ask for any rent rolls or occupancy—

A. We did.

Q. —reports?

Q. (By Mr. Peabody) And who did you ask?

A. Colonial Properties.

Q. Did you get any?

A. No, we did not.

Q. Did you ask for any income statements?

A. We did.

Q. (By Mr. Peabody) And who did you ask?

A. Colonial Properties.

Q. Did you get any?

A. No. They were all being updated.

Q. (By Mr. Peabody) When you asked, were you ever promised to be given any?

A. Yes.

Q. (By Mr. Peabody) When did you expect to get those?

A. We expected to get them before our contract was denied.

As I mentioned previously, if the sellers tell you they spent money on renovating units, they should not only be able to show you the units that they remodeled; they should be able to provide itemized financials that include expenses such as paint, appliances, and fixtures. Double-check every piece of information you're given. Names on rent rolls compared to leases, names on rent rolls from one month to the next, the number of utility bills versus the number of tenants. If a seller claims to have invested money in the property, it should show up on the P&L, tax returns, and canceled checks.

Ask the sellers or the sellers' agent what type of improvements they've done over the last year or two on the property, then compare their statements with the expenses on their profit and loss statement. If they tell you they've remodeled ten units, ask to see them. If they look nice, but they are only reporting $2,000 in expenses on their financials, this does not add up. Either one thing or the other is true but not both.

TIP 45

Be leery of sellers or their agents that have trouble producing financials.

Q. (By Mr. Peabody) Okay. Did you make an offer on the property for Mr. Sanchez?

A. We did.

Q. Okay. And how quickly did you do that after you saw the property?

A. That day and the day after.

Q. Okay. So even without that information, was Mr. Sanchez interested—still interested in buying the Crestview?

A. Most definitely. He wanted to put a contract in so he wouldn't lose the property.

Q. Okay.

A. And then, at that time, we were going to ask for all the financial statements.

Q. Okay.

Q. (By Mr. Peabody) And how—how soon after your visit to the Crestview Apartments did you start calling to ask for that financial information?

A. I remember it was on a weekend.

A. We started calling on Monday.

Q. (By Mr. Peabody) Okay.

Q. (By Mr. Peabody) Did you call to ask for that—did you call Colonial Properties to ask for that information more than once?

A. Yes.

Q. (By Mr. Peabody) Do you know how many times you called?

A. Three, four, five. I mean, it was on a daily basis.

Q. And for what—

Q. (By Mr. Peabody) For what period of time did you make those calls?

A. A whole week, week and a half.

Q. (By Mr. Peabody) Okay. What were you told about the availability of the kinds of financial information you were trying to get?

A. They were all being updated.

Q. (By Mr. Peabody) Okay. Were you given any information about how long it would take that update to be completed?

A. They told me within three to four days they would have everything to me. And three and four days passed, and I never received anything.

Q. (By Mr. Peabody) Okay. What was the response when you called or what did you ask when you called again?

A. I think I got on their nerves, so they canceled my contract because I was asking too many questions.

While it is easier to explain not having the current year's financials, the sellers should have had the documents used to create the prior year's tax returns. If a seller or their brokers are not immediately able to produce an audited financial statement or at the very least a copy of the Schedule E of their tax return this should be suspect and you should not proceed with this transaction.

TIP 46

Request an open records incident report from the local police department. If any officers' names or badge numbers appear on the report, interview them.

At this point, Michael and I still felt we needed more witnesses and started requesting any open records requests we could. The first we requested was a copy of the police incident reports for the Crestview Apartments from May 2006 until November 2006. This, incidentally, coincided with the period of time that Davis and Brewer held the listing on the property. Again, what we received should have been surprising, but it was not. There were nearly three hundred incident reports on the property from domestic violence, shootings, and drug trafficking. Michael then went about sorting out the badge numbers of the officers that responded to the majority of these calls. The officers that were on the property most frequently were Sam Wright and Walter Acevedo. After numerous calls to the police department, we were finally able to get these two officers to agree to an interview as to what they encountered while on the premises. The affidavit they provided to our attorney included the accounts of the apartments at the Crestview Apartments. The units were in uninhabitable condition, including, but not limited to, Sheetrock torn down to the studs, the presence of used hypodermic needles, and human feces on the floor. These were certainly not the conditions of the units we inspected while considering the purchase of the property. Again, the timeline of the officers' visits coincided directly with the listing period Colonial Properties had with the Fengs.

According to an affidavit given by Walter Acevedo of Corpus Christi PD on March 25, 2010:

"On various occasions, I responded to calls from residents of the Crestview Apartments. Most of those calls were from people living in the buildings at the front of the complex closest to Butler Road. Very few calls came from the back units, and it became apparent that was because very few of those units were occupied. These calls were mostly to report fights and drug activity. I realized, after responding to the calls, that the buildings farthest from Butler Road, those in the back, were mostly, if not completely, vacant. I specifically remember only one unit in that back building being occupied, by a woman on the bottom story. I believe she may have been a person who did cleanup at the Crestview Apartments. Many units had nothing on the windows or even had broken windows, and it was clear from the outside that the units in those buildings in the back were mostly vacant.

"Some of the calls were to report drug activity at the property. The property was a drug haven at that time. In investigating those calls, I would try to find the people who had been reported to be selling or using drugs and would go around to the back buildings of the complex. Many of those units had broken windows and were open. I sometimes entered those units, looking for suspects, and find those units filled with trash, including drug paraphernalia. Some were moldy, and had human feces on the floors. The smell in them was terrible, and they were not habitable."

The back buildings, Officer Acevedo noted, were vacant and covered with everything from drug paraphernalia to human feces, which, incidentally, was also the same building that sat right in front of the boarded-up pool. The same pool that both Isaac and Garrett admitted to being in front of but could not recall seeing all the abandoned units.

Officer Sam Wright observed many of the same things as Officer Acevedo in the affidavit he gave on March 25, 2010:

"Throughout 2006, I often was called to the Crestview Apartments. In addition, my usual patrols took me near the Crestview Apartments frequently. From the beginning of 2006 and through the summer and fall, the Crestview Apartments were in bad condition. The back two buildings were mostly vacant, with only one or two families living in those entire buildings. This was apparent to me because at night I would see that there would be no lights on in those units, while lights could be seen in other units. Also, no people would be outside near those units, as there were at the other apartment units at the Crestview Apartments. There were broken windows in many of those apartments in the back two buildings. I could see into those units from the outside of them, and it was apparent that they were vacant.

"When I would be called to the Crestview Apartments at that time, it would often be because of reports of drug activity. I frequently observed people smoking what appeared to be marijuana, and those people would run away when I approached. Those people would scatter and run to other apartment complexes in the neighborhood. They would leave behind drug paraphernalia. In responding to these calls, I also noticed that many of the units at the Crestview Apartments were vacant, but had been broken into and had broken windows. Those units were dirty, and trash had been left in them. Sometime in the fall of 2006, I noticed that the Crestview Apartments had been painted, and their condition began to improve slightly."

Officer Wright also noted that late in the listing period, the Crestview was painted. This occurred just prior to my first visit to the property. One of our contentions had always been that neither Michael nor I had been to the property before it was cleaned up. We never had the benefit of seeing the scribbled rent rolls the Fengs used to keep track of their collections. We were never privy to these things, but Garrett and Isaac were.

TIP 47

Talk to your competition. Go around the block and interview the managers of neighboring complexes regarding the tenant base, crime, and management at your property of interest. Ask about the history of the property. Were there things about this property's past that would be of interest to you? No matter what is reported to you by the sellers and their agents, your property did not exist in a bubble!

In the midst of all our misfortune, we did have some periods of good luck. Our manager, Harry Little, was fed up with the revolving door of renting units, evicting tenants, repairing units, re-renting units, evicting tenants, etc., not to mention that his vehicle was stolen right out of the parking lot of the complex. He was on the verge of quitting. In order to cover our bases should Harry decide to quit, I took out an ad for a resident manager on Craig's List and received only one response. It was from Juanita Suarez, who happened to have managed the Moon Palace Apartments from March 2006 through November 2006, which coincided almost perfectly with the Colonial Properties listing period. The Moon Palace Apartments coincidently shared a back fence with the Crestview Apartments, and Juanita's apartment overlooked the entire back part of the Crestview for nine months.

I called Juanita, and after a few minutes interviewing her over the phone I realized that Juanita had a lot more value to us as a witness than as an apartment manager. She was a material witness as to the conditions of the Crestview Apartments prior to me and Michael visiting the property. I asked

Juanita if she'd be willing to share her accounts of the Crestview to our attorney under oath, and she agreed.

So on Friday, November 6, 2009, we deposed Juanita Suarez. The following are some key excerpts from that testimony. The questions were being asked by our attorney, Harlan Peabody. Harlan began by establishing where the Moon Palace Apartments were in relation to the Crestview Apartments, and in particular where Juanita lived.

Q. Will you please state your name?
A. Juanita Suarez.
Q. Ms. Suarez, in 2006, what did you do for a living?
A. I was apartment manager for Moon Palace Apartments.
Q. And where are the Moon Palace Apartments?
A. 2540 Hemlock, Corpus Christi, Texas.
Q. Are they near the Crestview Apartments?
A. Behind.
Q. When you say *behind*, are they immediately next door?
A. Yes, sir, next door. It's just behind the apartments. We're in the front, and they're on the side of the building—of Butler Road. So, yes, we're behind—we're behind them.

Juanita went on to describe her position at the Moon Palace Apartments and the period in which she worked there.

Q. Okay. How long had you worked at the Moon Palace Apartments in 2006?
A. From March of 2006 until 11-15 of '06.
Q. That was the term of your employment there?
A. Employment.
Q. Okay. And you may have said this, but what was your job at the Moon Palace Apartments?
A. I was apartment manager.
Q. Did you live at the Moon Palace Apartments?
A. Yes, sir.
Q. Had you been in the apartment management business before you worked at Moon Palace?
A. Yes, sir.

Q. For how long?

A. Seven years, actually, more or less, an apartment manager.

Juanita recounted her memories of the condition of the Crestview Apartments:

Q. Okay. In 2006, in March of 2006, when you—when you started working at the Moon Palace Apartments, would you describe the general condition of the Crestview Apartments? Would you like me to give you as a percentage or as—well, just what was the physical condition of the buildings?

A. Actually, it was a lot of, like, some apartments were boarded up at the time. Some units didn't have blinds, but it was, like, the back patio window was broken.

Harlan tried to get Juanita to establish how many of the sixty-six units were visibly vacant and boarded up.

Q. Okay. If you don't know specifically which ones were boarded up after—after the years that have passed, do you know roughly how many were?

A. Well, roughly, I think it was through the four whole apartments, it was, like, maybe, ten apartments that—that some of them were boarded up, and some were the empty units, like, they had no curtains in it that you could see.

Q. No—no curtains. Is that what you said?

A. No. No blinds, you know.

Q. Okay.

A. No blinds.

Juanita's viewpoint of the condition of the exterior of the property was not much better.

Q. Okay. And then, generally, what about the condition of the property? Was it clean?

A. No, sir.

Q. Okay. Can you tell me what you saw?

A. Mainly, around the Dumpster, there's a lot of trash going on there. There was a lot of grass. I know that the manager—the owner was only once or once only one person that was doing everything, working really hard, but it was a lot of stuff, like, trash around the buildings.

Q. What condition was the paint in?

A. I would say fair.

Harlan went on to get Juanita to provide an estimate of the occupancy during her tenure as the manager of the Moon Palace Apartments:

Q. Okay. From your observations of the Crestview Apartments in the beginning of 2006, in March of 2006, do you have any estimate of how many units there were occupied?

A. I would put a percentage. It would be probably, maybe, no more than 70 percent.

Q. Okay. And how do you know that? What sort of—

A. I have—

Q. —things would you observe that would lead you to have that conclusion?

A. I have—I have friends that live there. Some of my old tenants was also— they were living there, and I visit them. That was—that was my intention of going to visit. I was—when I didn't start—I stopped working for the property, I meant to go rent an apartment there with Crestview, and I had seen their apartment.

Q. So you considered renting an apartment at Crestview, is that what you're saying?

A. That was my only chance—choice—that I had.

Q. Uh-huh. And did you rent an apartment there?

A. No, sir.

Q. Okay. And what did you see that leads you to believe that the Crestview Apartments were no more than 70 percent occupied?

A. A lot of people were drinking outside.

Q. (By Mr. Peabody) It's okay. Go ahead and answer.

A. Okay. There were a lot of people drinking outside, hangouts, shoot- ings, always ambulance. Police officer was there, drugs going in section into section. I mean, I seen this from my apartment, too, what I've seen there.

Q. Could you see into the apartments and tell whether people were living in any of the individual units?

A. In some of the units that were empty, yes, you can. You can—you can figure out that that was an empty unit.

Q. Did the conditions that you've described to us change between March and November of 2006? For example, you mentioned units being boarded up in March. Did that change over time that year in 2006?

A. I didn't—I didn't think it changed that much, because, I mean, as I was working for the company, I looked into the property there, but I didn't see hardly any changes within the time that I was there, not as extremely changed. I know they were painting the apartments. I seen that they were doing that change, but the insides or—no, sir.

Q. Okay. Did any of the boarded-up units, did the boards come down over the course of that year?

A. Not to my knowledge.

Q. In the later part of 2006, what would have been your estimate of how many units were occupied in the Crestview Apartments?

A. It would be my—still my 70 percent.

Harlan's line of questioning now turned to the crime that Juanita witnessed at the property.

Q. Okay. You mentioned that there were people hanging out and described some—some criminal activity. What did you see, in terms of criminal activity, at the Crestview Apartments?

A. There was—at one time, there was—I was in my apartment, apartment, which is back up behind the property. There's a gate between us, between the property—their property and my property. I was; there were some shootings going on. There was two guys shooting at each other. And I came out, and there was, like, gunshots, so we all went back.

Q. Uh-huh. Generally, did you notice anything else like that?

A. Just, like, the drug activity going out.

Q. And what did you see when you say "drug activity"?

A. Marijuana, smoking outside, you know, you could see cars going in and, you know, out, they come out, you know, just straight ahead. They'll just go in and what they're coming for. And the guy would stand up outside on the back building, which is the five—in the 500 building, and they would be right there, they would exchange whatever they're exchanging, and they would leave.

Q. Okay. Did that occur at the apartments you were managing?

A. Yes, sir.

Q. Okay.

A. Between the gate, their property, and my property, they would do exchanges there. They would park by the Dumpster. The guy would come over there, and they would do it. And I would call the cops on them.

TIP 48

Get feedback on the property from people other than the sellers and their agents!

Talk to service people that called on the property, such as neighbors, the mailman, the UPS driver, the pest exterminator, the police department, city inspectors, the insurance agents, or anyone that might have an unbiased opinion on the property you are considering to purchase. Ask them about noise, domestic violence, theft, and drugs that might be present in the complex. Talk to your tenants. I did this on one occasion at another property and found the on-site manager was charging the tenants $50 more than what he was reporting to the owner.

Your best witnesses could possibly be any one other than the seller or their agents!!

TIP 49

Don't do what we did!

Accept nothing at face value!

    Don't rely exclusively on the sellers or their agents!

SUMMARY

So, in summary in the summer of 2004 just prior to the Fengs' purchase, Crestview Apartments had been decimated by a hurricane. The roof was torn off the 700 building and was uninhabitable. According to the rent rolls of Janie Sinclair, the owner of the property prior to the Fengs, the Crestview Apartments at the time she turned over the keys in October 2004 was only 50 percent occupied.

Isaac Davis admitted he had been trying to get the listing on the Crestview from Janie, and if that was the case, it is reasonable to assume he was on the property at the time Janie wanted to sell.

In 2006, when Isaac did get the listing from the Fengs, he passed on a profit and loss statement to us stating that the building was 95 percent occupied. This financial statement commenced in January 2005, which was just two months after the Fengs closed on the property. A property that they admitted under oath was only 50 percent occupied. This stellar improvement on the occupancy at Crestview would have meant that the roof of the destroyed 700 building would have had to have been repaired and 29 vacancies would have had to have been filled in less than sixty days in order for the P&L Isaac gave us to be true. Is this impossible, no; improbable, yes.

We also discovered that Barney Taylor of Huckabee & Associates did get the listing from Janie Sinclair. We also found out that sometime between October 2004 and the time we went into escrow with the Fengs, Barney left Huckabee and started working in the same Colonial Properties office with Isaac and Garrett. Is it believable that the topic of the Crestview Apartments and the condition it was in when Barney sold the building never came up in the Colonial Properties office?

According to the affidavits of Officers Wright and Acevedo, and the testimony of Juanita Suarez, the property was between 50 and 70 percent occupied all the way up until July 2006, when Davis and Brewer took the listing on the property from the Fengs. These units, according to the testimonies of Officers Wright and Acevedo, Juanita Suarez, and Jenna Valdez were still boarded up and vacant well into 2006 and coincided with the entire listing period the Fengs had with Colonial Properties.

The 700 building, which by all accounts was completely vacant, sat right in front of the abandoned swimming pool that both Isaac and Garrett admitted to seeing during their visit to the property in both their depositions. In spite of being right in front of the buildings while they were looking at the pool nothing was mentioned about the boarded up windows and the obvious vacancies yet they did not see any reason to doubt the Fengs claim that the building was operating at 95% occupancy? The 700 building comprised ten of the sixty-six units, or roughly 15 percent of units in the complex, so already without even studying the financials, the observed occupancy, presuming all the other units were not only occupied but current with their rent, would put the occupancy well below the 95 percent that the Feng's claimed.

The Fengs, who had little knowledge of computers, and in particular Excel spreadsheets, were at the very least given a template by the agents so they could turn the scribbled rent rolls they used into sophisticated spreadsheets which would give any prospective buyer the impression that these documents were created by a professional accountant or bookkeeper, and as such, believable.

While during Brewer's and Davis's depositions they swore that they only provided the Feng's with templates, which included the titles filled out for each category (i.e., name, unit number, deposit amount, lease expiration, etc.), but it was the Fengs that completed them. June, on the other hand, admitted under oath that her financials were falsified and that the reported income was bolstered in order to get a better price on the building. June also testified that she did not recognize some of the information on the rent rolls even though she was the one who supposedly created it. Davis and Brewer stated under oath that they only provided a blank template to the Fengs, while June stated that the agents created the rent rolls from information she gave them. Which was it?

June's testimony reinforced our suspicions that the Fengs had not created the data. Our research of the metadata in the Excel spreadsheets and PDFs we had been given confirmed that all of the rent rolls and profit and loss statements were generated on Davis's and Brewer's computers; nothing was created on the Fengs' computers.

As we plowed through the volumes of material we were given through discovery, we found copies of handwritten rent rolls that the Fengs actually used that contained *only* unit numbers and payments. The Fengs' rent rolls were written on tablets, and in most cases they were discarded at the end of each month in favor of a new blank sheet of paper. No history of rent rolls was retained by the Fengs. If this was true, how is it that we were provided six months of financials when we made our offer on the property?

Michael and I were provided elaborate 10 column rent rolls for several months of prior rental history yet the Feng's claimed they never kept rent rolls from one month to the next. The Feng's could not produce one rent roll from their computer and in fact when confronted with the rent rolls they allegedly created they did not recognize them. The metadata from the spreadsheets showed that at least some or all of them were created on Davis and Brewers computers. During discovery we were provided with a handwritten profit and loss statement which appears to be the basis for which the rent rolls and profit loss statement that was used to establish the asking price for the Crestview (See "Doodle" in the appendix).

As we only had forty-five days to comb over the volumes of carefully prepared financial statements given to us by Colonial Properties during our due diligence period, we had to accept that what we were given was true and accurate. Later, during the months leading up to the trial, we had a lot more time to go over the financials we were given. The rent rolls we were provided evidenced tenants in a unit one month and then later found to disappear the next month. The same tenant later reappeared the next month only in another unit, then they were gone only to reappear the next month in another apartment.

So, in conclusion we have a property that was witnessed by two Corpus Christi police officers, the manager of the apartment building next door, a city code official and a seasoned real estate agent over a a a period of six months. This was a building that was so littered in trash and abandoned vehicles it was cited a nuisance for trash. A property so crime ridden that it had over 300 incident reports by the local police department. A complex which was so low on occupancy that the owner opted to board up units rather than to fix them up and rent them to new tenants.

This was a property that was offered at the same time by two seasoned agents that admittedly evaluated over 200 apartment buildings as "one of their best cash flowing properties" in the area.

This was a complex that was visited in October of 2006 returned in December 2006 to the Crestview with a new client who wanted to see the complex. Jenna's client, in spite of her warning about the condition of the property, insisted on visiting the Crestview.

What she witnessed and testified to was a complete metamorphosis of the property. The boards that were covering the windows had been replaced with mini-blinds, the building had been freshly painted, and all the abandoned vehicles and trash had been removed from the property. The property now looked as though it could have supported the type of revenue the agents had reported.

Unfortunately for us, two out-of-state buyers, we were already in negotiations with Colonial Properties to get this property under contract thinking we were getting the deal of the century.

Every one of our witnesses noted the number of units that had boards on the windows and some noted that the entire back two buildings on the property were vacant which were incidentally directly in front of the decommissioned swimming pool that both agents admitted to seeing. Each of these witnesses also noted the vacancies over a prolonged period of time which coincided directly with the time Brewer and Davis had the listing agreement with the Fengs.

The Crestview had 66 units and with 10-12 boarded up units this would have put the occupancy somewhere between 81-84%. This is not even taking into account the vacancies that probably existed in units which did not have boards over the windows. Without a second thought these two agents passed along rent rolls showing the property was performing at 95% occupancy for two solid years. The difference in income to us at this level alone was between $6000-8000 per month. By the time Michael and I arrived at the property these units were now occupied, probably by anyone that could fog up a mirror.

Is it believable that the agents working for Colonial Properties never came on the property or if they had did they not see the boarded up units, the trash, the abandoned vehicles?

Is it reasonable the Feng's were able to pull off the fraud of the century alone? Is it possible that in spite of the fact that the Brewer and Davis analyzed over 200 apartment complexes that they were duped by the Fengs? Is it possible that the Feng's agents believed they had no duty to the public to pass along financial statements that were obviously contrived? Did they have a duty to the public even if they did not have a fiduciary responsibility to the buyers? Did they have an experts knowledge of rental property? Did they have firsthand knowledge of the condition of the property prior to marketing it?

Weren't Davis and Brewer on the property at the same time as Corpus

Christi police officers? Didn't they walk in front of the same buildings as our witnesses which they described as having boarded-up windows and units that were vacant and unfit for human habitation? If they had been on the Crestview grounds wouldn't they would have witnessed the same abandoned vehicles that caused the Corpus Christi Health Department to cite the Fengs. Wasn't Garrett not only a real estate broker but a trained property manager and owned more than one multifamily complex himself?

How could such hard evidence of a nonperforming asset be overlooked by two experienced multifamily agents? How could it unless they knew that the issue with the vacancies and the boards would all need to be removed prior to marketing of this property? The fact that the boarded-up and vacant units were there was proof enough that the historical financials were fraudulent, and the Crestview was not "the cash-flowing machine" for the previous two years that they advertised.

During his deposition Isaac stated that the units "were cleaner than he expected".

What did he expect? Was he taking into account the hypodermic needles and human feces on the floors of the vacant units the Corpus Christi PD testified to?

What we also found interesting from Isaac's testimony was that he visited five or six vacant units. These, according to Isaac, were a "sampling of the vacant units," which would lead you to believe there were more that he did not visit. So presuming the Fengs lived in one unit, which would make the occupancy level at 90 percent or less, just from the units that Isaac admitted that he saw. If you recall, Isaac reported to us in his marketing flyer that the occupancy level for the property was consistently at 95 percent over two years. How many more vacant units was there that Isaac did not see?

Garrett and Isaac believed that they never had any duty to us because they were the Feng's agents even if they could see with their own eyes that the financial information they were passing on was false. What they failed to recognize was they still had a legal obligation not to create statutory fraud and were they conspiring to commit a crime through either omission or admission of a material fact, they too were guilty.

Armed with all of this great evidence, as well as the testimony of several credible witnesses, we felt we had a better than even shot of incriminating Garrett and Isaac in the fraud. We had previously settled with the Fengs. The Fengs, as you recall, had no evidence of any of the proceeds they made on this sale in any of their accounts. They even went so far as to hire a bankruptcy attorney to convince us that they had successfully moved all of their holdings into accounts they had in the People's Republic of China. The Fengs, through their attorney, convinced us that if we did not settle with them, they would file bankruptcy in the United States and flee the country for China, where our money was waiting for them. Feeling we had no alternative, we accepted their settlement offer of $150,000, which was a fraction of the $1,385,000 we owed the bank. We banked on the fact that the Fengs, who were now protected from any further damage from the lawsuit, would roll over on Garrett and Isaac.

EPILOGUE

On May 10, 2010, Michael and I entered the Nueces County Courthouse to begin our civil trial against the Feng's. It was nearly four years since we had first walked on the grounds of the Crestview Apartments. The lawyer and hired gun for Colonial Properties E&O carrier, named Hamilton Stone, with very little preparation, proceeded to discredit us, our witnesses, our legal defense, our managers, and our management of the property, and convinced the jury that Isaac and Garrett were innocent victims of the Fengs' fraudulent behavior. After six days, the jury came back with a verdict that the Fengs were 90 percent responsible and guilty of fraud and that Michael and I were, for some reason, 10 percent to blame, probably for not catching them in their lie.

Five years, $2.5 million in debt, and hundreds of hours of time invested in managing a losing property, not to mention the hundreds of hours compiling evidence in preparation for our day in court, could not be undone. For about a couple hours we felt totally lost. The time was spent, and the debt on our homes and credit cards was ours, and now with no short-term chance of recovery. Then it started to sink in that it was over. No more losing any more money, no more countless hours combing over discovery and depositions in order to make sure we captured every minute fact or detail. We could start down the long road of settling with our creditors and piecing our lives back together.

While we did not win our civil case, there was a small silver lining to this dark cloud. We took June Feng's deposition in which she admitted that she had falsified the financials we were given in order to sell the building for more money, and turned them over to Donny Sykes at the Nueces County DA's office. After another eighteen months, June was convicted of "Felony One, Execution of a Document through Deception (Fraud)." She was taken in handcuffs from in front of her new $300,000 house for which she somehow managed pay cash, in front of her neighbors where she pleaded with Donny to "let her sit in the front seat" so she would not be embarrassed in front of her neighbors.

June ultimately pled guilty and appeared in court with a handful of tenant witnesses, most of who had been allowed to live on the property rent free, the same tenants whom we ultimately evicted. The judge awarded us another $75,000 and gave June five years of probation. The Fengs netted nearly $750,000 after restitution and legal expenses.

Although we cannot prove it, less than a year after our civil trial, neither Garrett nor Isaac were employed at Colonial Properties, jobs both of them had held for several years. We have to believe that despite the fact that Colonial Properties had an obligation to defend them; the senior management knew that they had dodged a bullet and that these agents presented a liability.

Do I believe we were defrauded by the Fengs? I do. Do I believe the agents knew the information they were giving to us was false if not personally involved in creating it? I do. Do I feel that we should have deposed all the witnesses before the agents so that we would have been able to use their testimony in questioning the agents? I do. Do I believe we could have done a better job of presenting our case? I do. Do I believe the jury did not get it? I do. Were we bitter about losing? We were. We were for a while. As the days turned into weeks, and the weeks turned into months since the verdict was rendered, the bitterness began to fade, and we began to reflect on the lessons we learned from this ordeal. We learned not only about real estate, but we learned about ourselves.

In terms of real estate, we learned to not take anything at face value. We learned the meaning of "a penny wise and a pound foolish." It is a lot less expensive to not close on a deal unless you are confident that everything is as reported. We learned it is a lot less expensive to invest more time in the beginning doing your due diligence than it is trusting that a jury will get it right at the end. We also learned about the type of men we were. We didn't use what was happening to us to affect our values as men and as fathers. We did not use our financial problems as an excuse to not keep the promises we made to our families, our churches, or our careers. When everyone else told us to file for bankruptcy, we persevered and eventually found light at the end of the tunnel. We did not back down to the fight. We faced big government, big banks, politicians, the FBI, our senator and big corporate attorneys knowing these were defining moments for us and that years from now our children would know the type of men their fathers were. At the end of the day, when this was all over, there was a great deal of satisfaction that we saw this ordeal through to the end without compromising who we were.

This was not just a lesson in real estate. It was a lesson that Michael and I learned about ourselves. This story is only a fraction of what we encountered. This story does not include how Hurricane Ike decimated the property and how our insurance agent never purchased the hurricane insurance for which we paid him, how we attempted to sell the property to an out-of-state investor on contract, and how he absconded with $32,000 in rent from our decimated property and then fled town.

Michael, who was indifferent to religion, found faith. I, on the other hand, who was raised in the church, had my faith rocked. We both found our knees. We learned that money isn't as important as we thought it was. We learned the value of relationships, savoring moments, being present, and living in the moment. I don't believe we would have learned the life lessons we did had we been victorious and been awarded a large settlement.

Through the providence of God and our perseverance, we settled with all our creditors, much to the disbelief of our closest family, friends, and advisers. Michael and I, rather than blaming one another for our misfortune, became as two soldiers in a foxhole, each with the other's back. We developed a strong belief in ourselves that we could overcome any situation through what we learned by this experience.

Are we discouraging the reader from investing in real estate? No; in fact, quite the contrary. We believe that real estate is an excellent vehicle for creating wealth. We only caution prospective investors to do their due diligence while analyzing the value of property, to not accept anything at face value, and to check and double-check the information they are provided. It is a lot easier to pay your dues up front than it is to leave your fate to a jury.

Information Record

Name	████████████	Subject	████████
Organization	████████████████████	Telephone Business	
Address	████████████████████		

1966   Fax   **90%**

6.25 Acres   ~~electric~~ Other - spark

Date	Follow-up	Notes
		Submetered - Pitched - ok
		concrete - gated
		private patio - some
		1/1 17 670 ▯ $795
	TH	2/1.5 6 1,085 ▯ $585
		2/2 20 1,000 ▯ ~~$~~ $475
		2/2 10 1,100 ▯ $500
		3/2 10 1,500 ▯ $650
		2/2 2 1,220 ▯ $550
		3/2 1 1,500 ▯ $650

$29,000 / mo Collections

$11,000 - insurance - no deposit

©1997 Franklin Covey Co. Printed in USA   Original-CL 17428

Information Record

Name ████████████	Subject
Organization	Telephone · Business
Address	Home
	Fax
	Other

Date	Follow-up	Notes
		Tax 2?K
		LAl ⮕55K
		elec
		gas
		water
		Tax Tax $?00/mo
		Rtn $1k/mo
		Payrol $500/mo

Exhibit Doodle-This was the financial statement the agents were given when they took the listing. Exhibit 4 is what we were given.

Sep. 06

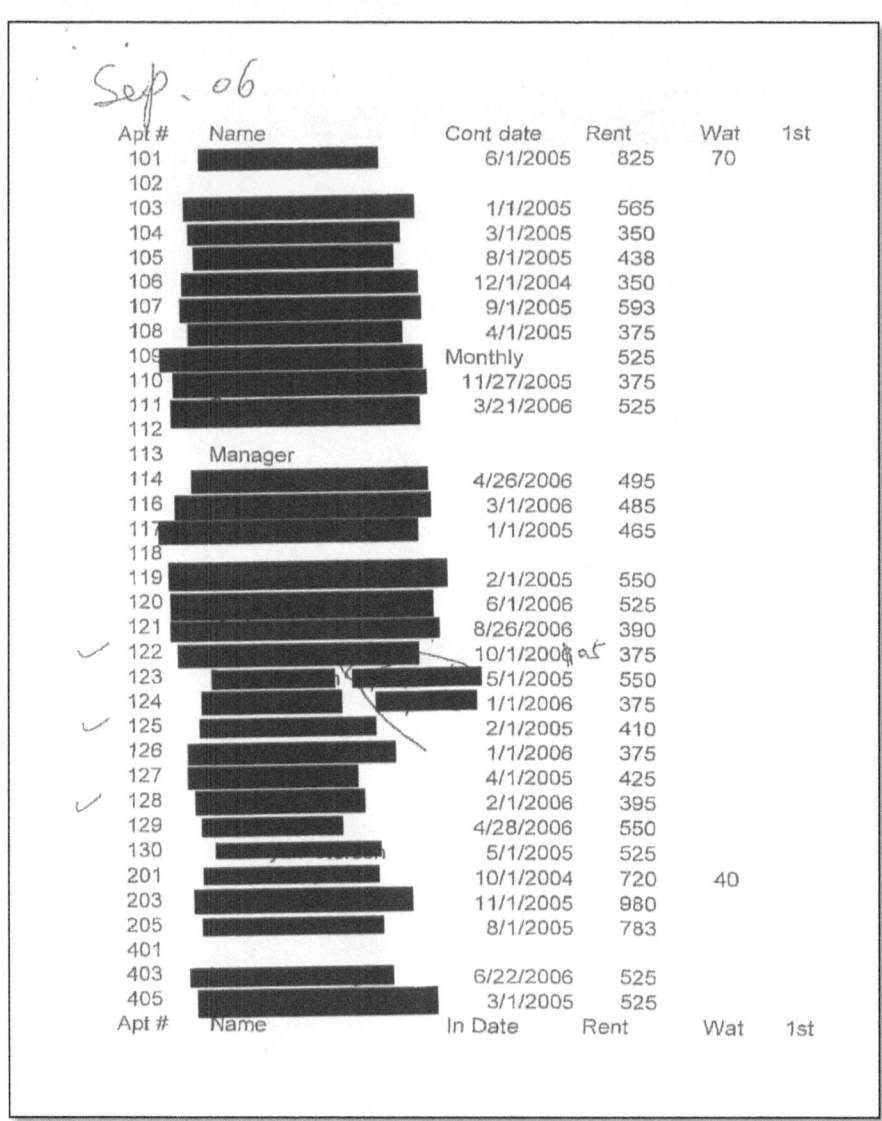

Apt #	Name	Cont date	Rent	Wat	1st
101	▮▮▮▮▮▮	6/1/2005	825	70	
102					
103	▮▮▮▮▮▮	1/1/2005	565		
104	▮▮▮▮▮▮	3/1/2005	350		
105	▮▮▮▮▮▮	8/1/2005	438		
106	▮▮▮▮▮▮	12/1/2004	350		
107	▮▮▮▮▮▮	9/1/2005	593		
108	▮▮▮▮▮▮	4/1/2005	375		
109	▮▮▮▮▮▮	Monthly	525		
110	▮▮▮▮▮▮	11/27/2005	375		
111	▮▮▮▮▮▮	3/21/2006	525		
112					
113	Manager				
114	▮▮▮▮▮▮	4/26/2006	495		
116	▮▮▮▮▮▮	3/1/2006	485		
117	▮▮▮▮▮▮	1/1/2005	465		
118					
119	▮▮▮▮▮▮	2/1/2005	550		
120	▮▮▮▮▮▮	6/1/2006	525		
121	▮▮▮▮▮▮	8/26/2006	390		
122	▮▮▮▮▮▮	10/1/2006 at	375		
123	▮▮▮▮▮▮	5/1/2005	550		
124	▮▮▮▮▮▮	1/1/2006	375		
125	▮▮▮▮▮▮	2/1/2005	410		
126	▮▮▮▮▮▮	1/1/2006	375		
127	▮▮▮▮▮▮	4/1/2005	425		
128	▮▮▮▮▮▮	2/1/2006	395		
129	▮▮▮▮▮▮	4/28/2006	550		
130	▮▮▮▮▮▮	5/1/2005	525		
201	▮▮▮▮▮▮	10/1/2004	720	40	
203	▮▮▮▮▮▮	11/1/2005	980		
205	▮▮▮▮▮▮	8/1/2005	783		
401					
403	▮▮▮▮▮▮	6/22/2006	525		
405	▮▮▮▮▮▮	3/1/2005	525		
Apt #	Name	In Date	Rent	Wat	1st

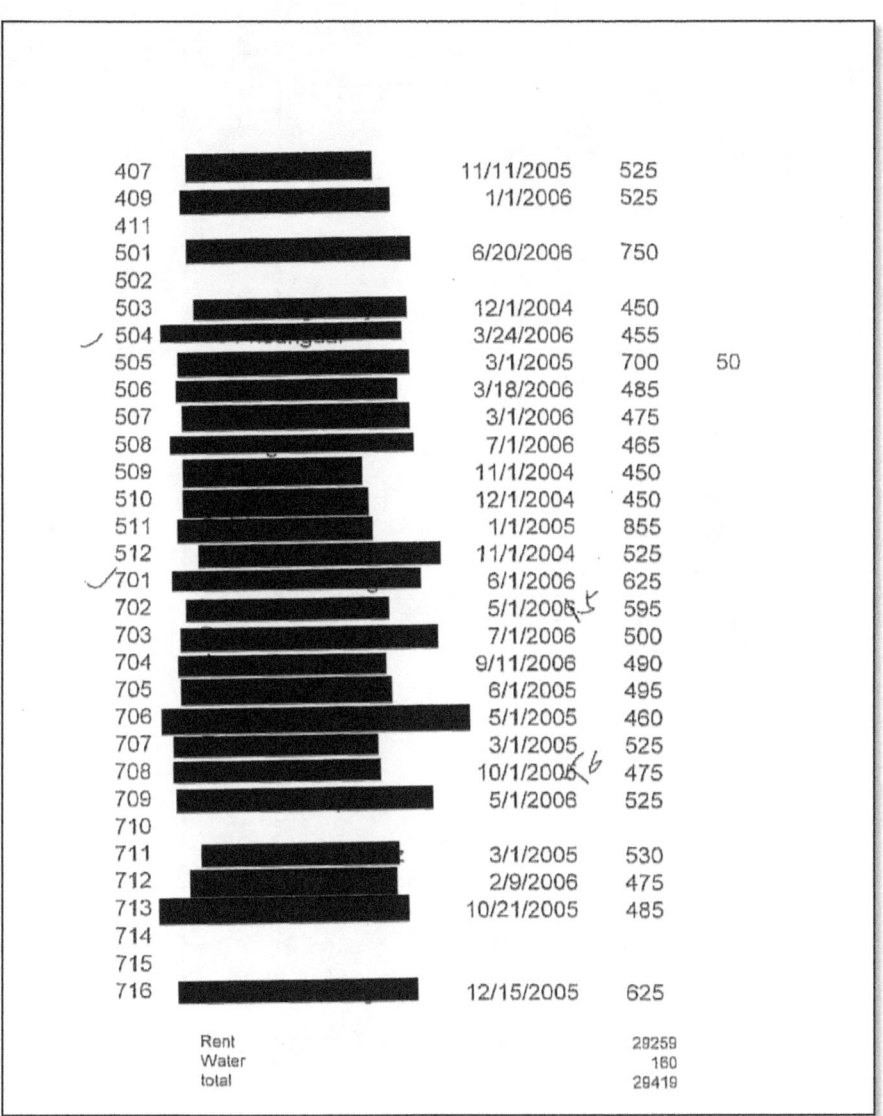

407		11/11/2005	525
409		1/1/2006	525
411			
501		6/20/2006	750
502			
503		12/1/2004	450
504		3/24/2006	455
505		3/1/2005	700	50
506		3/18/2006	485
507		3/1/2006	475
508		7/1/2006	465
509		11/1/2004	450
510		12/1/2004	450
511		1/1/2005	855
512		11/1/2004	525
701		6/1/2006	625
702		5/1/2005	595
703		7/1/2006	500
704		9/11/2006	490
705		6/1/2005	495
706		5/1/2005	460
707		3/1/2005	525
708		10/1/2005	475
709		5/1/2006	525
710			
711		3/1/2005	530
712		2/9/2006	475
713		10/21/2005	485
714			
715			
716		12/15/2005	625

Rent	29259
Water	180
total	29419

Exhibit 1-This was an example of the Feng's rent roll once the Crestview was on the market. According to the deposition the Feng's provided they would list a unit number on a piece of yellow legal pad and when the month was over they'd throw the paper away and while this rent roll was an improvement over what the Feng's used over during their ownership of their management compare this document with Exhibit.

2005 Profit Loss

	January	February	March	April	May	June	July	August	September	October	November	December	TOTAL
Income													
Rent	$27,532	$27,865	$28,126	$27,956	$28,121	$28,465	$28,755	$28,676	$28,764	$28,445	$28,055	$28,894	$339,654
Other Income	$683	$656	$578	$764	$672	$689	$675	$654	$664	$643	$672	$528	$7,978
Total Income	$28,215	$28,521	$28,704	$28,720	$28,793	$29,154	$29,430	$29,330	$29,428	$29,088	$28,727	$29,522	$347,632
Expenses													
Utilities	$4,108	$3,470	$3,923	$3,527	$3,399	$3,714	$4,574	$6,335	$4,726	$3,389	$6,420	$4,287	$51,872
R&M	$808	$905	$1,108	$875	$976	$1,250	$1,105	$1,280	$1,342	$1,012	$716	$1,125	$12,502
Wages	$600	$600	$600	$600	$600	$600	$600	$600	$600	$600	$600	$600	$7,200
Advertizing	$40	$40	$40	$40	$40	$40	$40	$40	$40	$40	$40	$40	$480
Insurance	0.00	0.00	0.00	0.00	0.00	0.00	0.00	0.00	0.00	$11,030	0.00	0.00	$11,030
Total Expenses	$5,556	$5,015	$5,671	$5,042	$5,015	$5,604	$6,319	$8,255	$6,708	$16,071	$7,776	$6,052	$83,084
NOI	$22,659	$23,506	$23,033	$23,678	$23,778	$23,550	$23,111	$21,075	$22,720	$13,017	$20,951	$23,470	$264,548

Exhibit 4–This was the Profit and Loss Statement that was given to us by the agents.

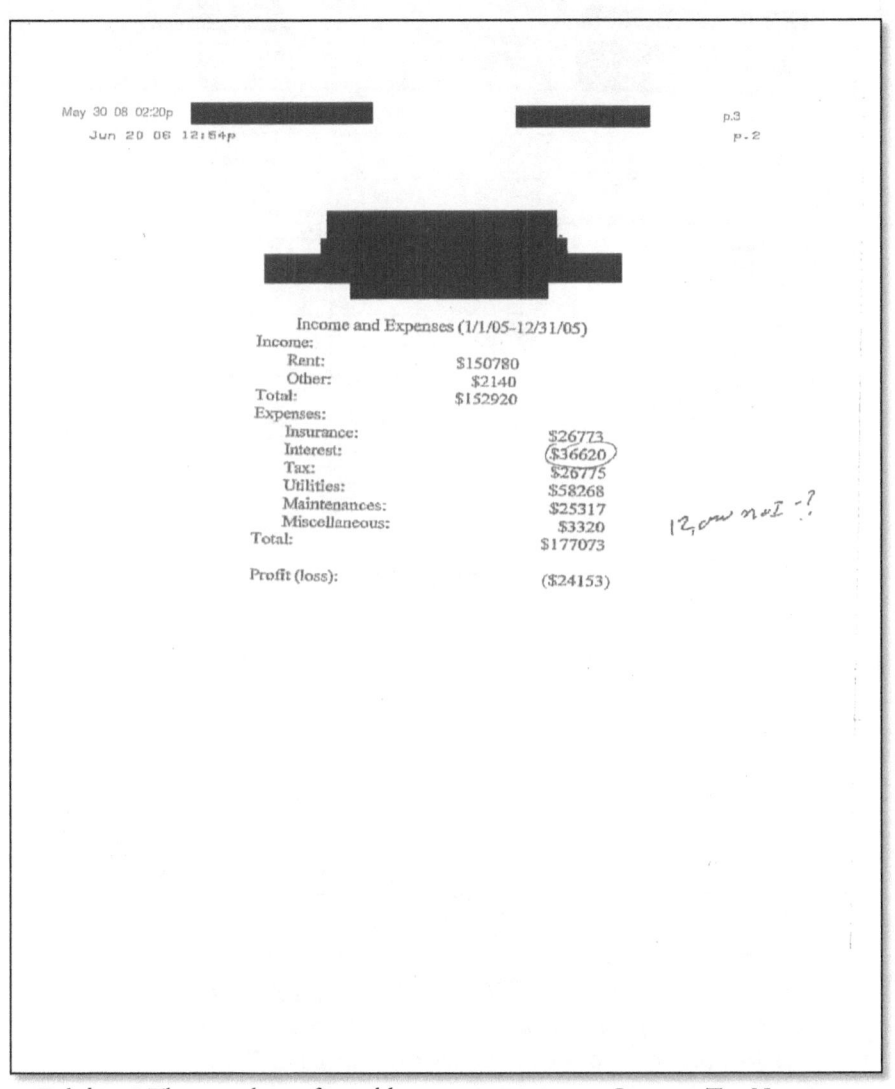

Income and Expenses (1/1/05–12/31/05)

Income:

    Rent: $150780

    Other: $2140

Total: $152920

Expenses:

    Insurance: $26773

    Interest: ($36620)

    Tax: $26775

    Utilities: $58268

    Maintenances: $25317

    Miscellaneous: $3320

Total: $177073

Profit (loss):   ($24153)

Exhibit 5-This was the profit and loss statement given to Property Tax Negotiators for 2005 in order for the Fengs to get their property taxes lowered. Compare these figures with those given to us in the due diligence period from Exhibit 4.

			Properties			
			A	B	C	D

Form 8825 — Rental Real Estate Income and Expenses of a Partnership or an S Corporation

► See instructions on back
► Attach to Form 1065, Form 1065-B, or Form 1120S.

2005

Employer identification number

1. Show the kind and location of each property. See page 2 to list additional properties.

A

B

C

D

			A	B	C	D
Rental Real Estate Income						
2 Gross rents		2	146,540			
Rental Real Estate Expenses						
3 Advertising		3	720			
4 Auto and travel		4				
5 Cleaning and maintenance		5	7,315			
6 Commissions		6				
7 Insurance		7	11,256			
8 Legal and other professional fees		8	1,219			
9 Interest		9	43,039			
10 Repairs		10	11,155			
11 Taxes		11				
12 Utilities		12	65,258			
13 Wages and salaries		13				
14 Depreciation (see instructions)		14	23,606			
15 Other (list) ► See Statement 2		15	5,322			
16 Total expenses for each property. Add lines 3 through 15		16	168,890			

17 Total gross rents. Add gross rents from line 2, columns A through H 17   146,540

18 Total expenses. Add total expenses from line 16, columns A through H 18 (168,890)

19 Net gain (loss) from Form 4797, Part II, line 17, from the disposition of property from rental real estate activities 19

20a Net income (loss) from rental real estate activities from partnerships, estates, and trusts in which this partnership or S corporation is a partner or beneficiary (from Schedule K-1) 20a

 b Identify below the partnerships, estates, or trusts from which net income (loss) is shown on line 20a. Attach a schedule if more space is needed

 (1) Name   (2) Employer ID number

21 Net rental real estate income (loss). Combine lines 17 through 20a. Enter the result here and on:

 ● Form 1065 or 1120S: Schedule K, line 2, or
 ● Form 1065-B: Part I, line 4   21   -22,350

For Paperwork Reduction Act Notice, see back of form.   Form 8825 (2005)

Exhibit 6-This is the form 8825 from the Feng's 2005 tax return which we received during the discovery phase of our lawsuit which shows gross income of $146,540 with a loss of $22,500 as opposed to $339,654 in gross income and $264,568 profit reported in Exhibit 4 which we were given by the agents during the due diligence period of purchase of the Crestview.

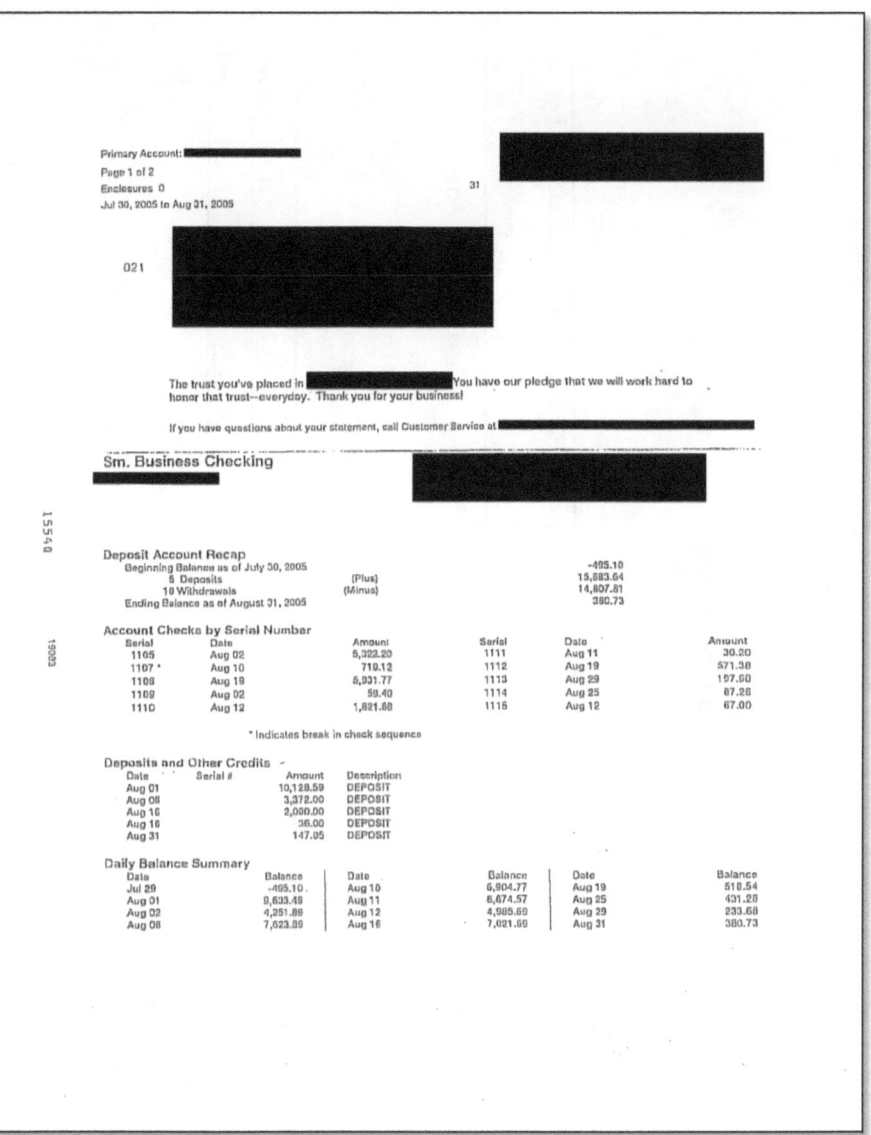

Primary Account:
Page 1 of 2
Enclosures 0
Jul 30, 2005 to Aug 31, 2005

31

021

The trust you've placed in ▓▓▓▓▓▓▓▓▓ You have our pledge that we will work hard to
honor that trust—everyday. Thank you for your business!

If you have questions about your statement, call Customer Service at ▓▓▓▓▓▓▓▓▓

Sm. Business Checking

15510

19083

Deposit Account Recap

Beginning Balance as of July 30, 2005		-495.10
5 Deposits	(Plus)	15,683.64
10 Withdrawals	(Minus)	14,807.81
Ending Balance as of August 31, 2005		380.73

Account Checks by Serial Number

Serial	Date	Amount	Serial	Date	Amount
1105	Aug 02	5,322.20	1111	Aug 11	30.20
1107 *	Aug 10	719.12	1112	Aug 19	571.38
1108	Aug 19	5,031.77	1113	Aug 29	197.90
1109	Aug 02	59.40	1114	Aug 25	87.26
1110	Aug 12	1,821.68	1115	Aug 12	67.00

* Indicates break in check sequence

Deposits and Other Credits

Date	Serial #	Amount	Description
Aug 01		10,128.59	DEPOSIT
Aug 08		3,372.00	DEPOSIT
Aug 16		2,000.00	DEPOSIT
Aug 16		36.00	DEPOSIT
Aug 31		147.05	DEPOSIT

Daily Balance Summary

Date	Balance	Date	Balance	Date	Balance
Jul 29	-495.10	Aug 10	6,904.77	Aug 19	510.54
Aug 01	9,633.49	Aug 11	6,874.57	Aug 25	431.28
Aug 02	4,251.89	Aug 12	4,985.69	Aug 29	233.68
Aug 08	7,623.89	Aug 16	7,021.69	Aug 31	380.73

*Exhibit 7-This is a typical bank statement of the Feng's. Each of them
was similar in nature. No one month had a deposit of more than
$18,000. In this particular month of July 2005 the Feng's reported on the
2005 P&L receipts for this month were $28,755 while the bank deposits
for the same month were only $15,683. A $13,000 difference!*

2006 Profit Loss

	January	February	March	April	May	June	July	August	September	October	November	December	TOTAL
Income													
Rent	$27,685	$28,135	$28,605	$26,454	$29,232	$28,767	$29,420	$29,258	$29,345	$29,695	$29,320	$29,855	$347,771
Other Income	$675	$756	$738	$620	$558	$672	$775	$658	$823	$847	$535	$632	$8,289
Total Income	$28,360	$28,891	$29,343	$29,074	$29,790	$29,439	$30,195	$29,916	$30,168	$30,542	$29,855	$30,487	$356,060
Expenses													
Utilities	$4,235	$3,957	$4,126	$4,295	$4,310	$4,286	$6,104	$4,948	$4,624	$6,251	$5,415	$4,758	$57,309
R&M	$875	$905	$1,045	$826	$655	$732	$755	$679	$780	$645	$695	$765	$9,557
Wages	$600	$600	$600	$600	$600	$600	$600	$600	$600	$600	$600	$600	$7,200
Advertizing	$40	$40	$40	$40	$40	$40	$40	$40	$40	$40	$40	$40	$480
Insurance										$9,750			$9,750
Total Expenses	$5,750	$5,502	$5,811	$5,761	$5,605	$5,658	$7,499	$6,267	$6,044	$17,286	$6,950	$6,163	$84,296
NOI	$22,610	$23,389	$23,532	$23,313	$24,185	$23,781	$22,606	$23,649	$24,124	$13,256	$22,905	$24,324	$271,764

Exhibit 11-This is the 2006 Profit and Loss statement that we were given during the due diligence period. The income and expenses are relatively the same as the 2005 statement.

Cash - Flow Report Jan - Aug 2004													
Monthly Cash Flow													
		Jan	Feb	Mar	Apr	May	Jun	Jul	Aug	Sept	Oct	Nov	Dec	yr income
Total Apts	66	15,067	15,603	13,215	13,025	13,141	13,062	13,880	13,560	13,232	12,687			136,472
Avail Apts	66													
Rental Inc	100%	42,695	42,695	42,695	42,695	42,695	42,695	42,695	42,695	42,695	42,695			at100%
Other Inc														
Concessions, Laundry		16.36	21.52	17.48	18.65	104.85	105.85	110.35	95.68	84.73	76.89			652
Total Income														137,124

Sinclair 2004 Income Statement-This was the final financial statement Janie Sinclair had prior to the sale of the Crestview Apartments to the Fengs in October of 2004. The property had been hit by a tornado in the second half of the year leaving the 700 building without a roof and completely vacant. The 700 building comprised 11% of the total number of units at the Crestview Apartments. Two years later the Feng's would report to us that the property was 95% occupied starting in January of 2005 just two months after this financial statement was created. It was also around this time Isaac Davis was attempting to get the listing from Sinclair. Isaac was also the one who provided us with the 2005 P&L showing the high occupancy. The property was less than 40% occupied in October of 2004.

www.ingramcontent.com/pod-product-compliance
Lightning Source LLC
Chambersburg PA
CBHW021952170526
45157CB00003B/952